THE VI

A Play

by
LADISLAS FODOR

SAMUEL FRENCH

LONDON
NEW YORK   TORONTO   SYDNEY   HOLLYWOOD

THE VIGIL

Produced at the Prince of Wales Theatre, London, on May 10th, 1948, with the following cast of characters:

(in the order of their appearance)

Mrs Haris—*the Charwoman* (a negress)	Ida Shepley
The Night Watchman	Hilary Pritchard
The Judge	Charles Cameron
The Prosecutor	Douglass Montgomery
The Defence Counsel	Barry K. Barnes
The Clerk of the Court	Reginald Barlow
The Gardener—*the Defendant*	Conrad Phillips
The Guard	
Esther—*a Country Girl*	Elizabeth Bird
Lucius—*a Soldier*	Walter Gotell
Mr Pinchas—*a Shopkeeper*	Frank Dunlop
Joseph—*a Wealthy Lawyer*	Ferdy Mayne
Lady Procula—*the Governor's Wife*	Marjory Hawtrey
Pontius Pilate—*the Governor*	Anthony Shaw
Saul—*a Deputy*	David Greene
Beulah—*a Barmaid*	Julie Mortimer
Sadoc—*a Private Detective*	Tony Quinn
Susannea—*a Housewife*	Katherine Blake
Thaddeus—*a Professor*	Richard Littledale
Magdalen—*a Convert*	Diana Churchill
Peter—*a Fisherman*	Philip Ray

SYNOPSIS OF SCENES

The action of the play passes in the Courthouse of any small town in the United States of America.

ACT I.   Good Friday night.

ACT II.   The following night.

ACT III.   The same night. Just before dawn.

Time—the present.

ACT 1

SCENE.—*The courtroom in the Courthouse of any small town in the United States of America. Good Friday evening.*

Back stage C. *are three large windows in a bay, affording a generous view of the town square; a white colonial church with its steeple etched against the sky, and the hills beyond, where violet shadows forecast the evening. There are doors* C. *of the walls* R. *and* L. *Set in the window bay up* C. *is a rostrum on which stands the* JUDGE's *desk and chair. A small rostrum, on which there is a chair for the witnesses, stands* L.C. *There is a small desk and chair for the* CLERK OF THE COURT *up* R.C.; *a table and chair for the* DEFENCE COUNSEL *down* R.; *and a table and chair for the* PROSECUTOR *down* L. *A chair for the* GUARD *stands up* R. *The jury box is assumed to be in the direction of the audience.*

(See the Ground Plan at the end of the Play.)

When the CURTAIN *rises,* MRS HARIS *is kneeling on the rostrum of the witness stand, with her back to the audience, and for a moment, she gives the illusion of praying, but actually, she is dusting the chair. The glow of the setting sun floods the windows up* C. MRS HARIS *is a negress in her late forties, and as she works she unconsciously hums a tune.*

MRS HARIS (*singing softly*).
  Nobody knows de trouble I've seen, Lord.
  Nobody knows but Jesus. . . .

(*The* NIGHT WATCHMAN *enters* R. *He is in his vigorous fifties. He jingles a bunch of keys.*)

WATCHMAN. Still at it, Mrs Haris? What's taking you so long?
MRS HARIS (*rising and turning*). Doin' my spring cleaning, Mr Woods. The place sure was a mess. (*She pauses and gives the chair a final flick with her duster.*) Goin' away for the holidays?
WATCHMAN (*easing* R.C.). Nope! This Easter I'm stuck.

(MRS HARIS *crosses to the table down* R. *and dusts it.*)

Gotta stay on the job. The super is gone up to the lake with the judge. Goin' to help him put the cabin in shape and give the boat a paint job.
MRS HARIS (*chuckling*). Air't it the beatenes' thing!

(*The* WATCHMAN *eases* C.)

Come Easter and the paintin' spirit gets 'em all. (*She devoutly polishes the table.*) 'Spect when the good Lord rises he wants to find everythin' spick and span.

(*The light is steadily fading.*)

WATCHMAN. No-one don't care whether the good Lord rises or not these days. It's just an excuse for a holiday. The young folk have all forgot what Easter's for.

MRS HARIS. Why, Mr Woods! What an awful thing to say. Does you really think the young folk have forgot the good Lord rises every Easter time? Why, if what you says is true, they've got an awful lot to explain when they meets the Lord on Judgement Day.

WATCHMAN (*moving to the door* R.). Come on, hurry it up—it's getting dark.

MRS HARIS. Late as that? (*She moves* C.) I'd better run down-stairs and straighten up my room. My daughter is comin' to town with the evenin' train. She's bringin' a baked ham and her new baby.

WATCHMAN. Sounds like the makings of a swell holiday. (*He locks the door* R.) Let's lock up and get out of here. (*He moves* C.)

MRS HARIS (*moving up* L.). Just a minute 'til I pick up my stuff. (*She picks up the mop, broom and dustpan, and moves to the door* L.)

WATCHMAN (*moving to her*). I'll take the pail.

(*He picks up the pail and moves to the door* L. *MRS HARIS exits and he follows her off, closes the door behind him and is heard to lock it. There is a finality in the sharp click of the lock. The courtroom is closed for the holidays. There is a deep silence. Outside, the night comes abruptly. Darkness takes over. During the black-out the* JUDGE, *the* PROSECUTOR, *the* DEFENCE COUNSEL, *the* CLERK OF THE COURT, *the* GARDENER, *and the* GUARD, *enter silently and quickly, and take their places. Then, after a pause heavy with tension, there is a dull thud as the* JUDGE *raps his gavel on his desk in the empty silence.*)

CLERK (*speaking into the void*). Hear ye, hear ye, hear ye! This Court is now in session.

(*At these words the scene gradually lights up and with the returning light, human figures take shape in the courtroom. They are just there, all the elements of a trial, materialized out of nothing. Though the circum-stances are mystifying, this is not a phantom trial. It is a real trial. The* JUDGE, *seated at his desk up* C., *with his silver-haired dignity, is real and of today. The* PROSECUTOR, *seated at his table down* L., *is a dark-haired man in his brilliant thirties. Sharp, intelligent, ambitious, he has a handsome, sarcastic profile. The* DEFENCE COUNSEL, *seated at his table down* R., *matches him perfectly, mentally as in stature. The two opponents are exactly the same age, possibly from the same law school. The* COUNSELLOR, *however, is the brighter figure, with a face alight*)

with enthusiasm; obviously a man of high principles; for it is evident
that his client is very poor. The defendant, a simple GARDENER, *is*
seated above the COUNSELLOR. *He wears a lumberjack shirt and blue*
overalls. He has the calloused hands of a toiler and his weatherbeaten
face is covered with a matted beard. It is very apparent that he has no
idea of court procedure. The CLERK OF THE COURT *is seated at his*
desk up R.C., *and the* GUARD *is standing up* R. *At the moment, the*
preliminaries are over and the State is about to present its case.)

PROSECUTOR (*rising and moving* C.). May it please the Court—
ladies and gentlemen of the Jury. On the night of April eight, in a
quiet garden on a hillside, a crime was committed. The first part
of this night passed peacefully. Nothing revealed that the crime
had already taken shape in the mind of a man. Only when the
stars faded away did the gardener, the defendant in this action,
leave his cottage to embark upon a strange errand. In the nearby
stable he untied a mule, led it up to the well, and harnessed it to
the wheel of the water pump. (*He paces a few steps* R. *and* L. *as he*
continues.) Leaving the beast to its chore of filling up the reservoir,
the defendant proceeded along the path until he reached the
upper end of the garden, where the rocks of the hillside blocked
his way. This was the place. Shrouded by mist and darkness the
gardener went to work. He dislodged a great stone firmly set in
the soil, entered the tomb behind it, and removed the body of a
Jewish teacher called Jesus of Nazareth. (*He halts and faces the*
audience.) Ladies and gentlemen of the Jury, though there is a
vast distance in time and space, between the crime and this
present-day trial before the People's Court, we open the case with
unabated determination, as we open it every nightfall of Good
Friday, in the courtroom of every modern man's mind. We have
before us the facts as clearly as ever, and we will continue to trace
them. The State will prove to the Jury what really happened in
that garden, before sunrise, on the third day after the body was
reposed. (*He resumes his pacing.*) It requires a great deal of restraint
for the State to narrow itself to the presentation of the bare facts.
But, for the time being, let us follow the gardener step by step.
Emerging from the tomb with his burden, he returned to the well
where, in the meantime, the reservoir had been filled. In the bed
of a drained water canal, he dug a hole, buried the body, and
levelled the soil over it. Then he opened the gates of the reservoir.
Water flooded the canal, washing away all trace of the burial—
and when the sun rose that first day of the week, the tomb was
empty. Who rolled away the stone? An angel from heaven, perhaps? (*He halts and faces the audience.*) No, ladies and gentlemen.
The State will prove that it was the gardener, he and no other.
Therefore, the State accuses the defendant, Yahuda Jacobson, of
snatching the body of Jesus of Nazareth on the night of April
eight—burying it in an unmarked grave—and by this malicious

scheme, perpetrating the greatest fraud of mankind. (*He moves to his chair down* L. *and sits.*)

(*A shocked silence grips the courtroom. After a few moments, the* DEFENCE COUNSEL *rises abruptly.*)

COUNSELLOR. Your Honour, the Defence does not wish to make an opening statement at this time. (*He sits.*)
JUDGE. Proceed with the evidence.

(*The* PROSECUTOR *rises and moves to the witness stand* L.C.)

PROSECUTOR. Miss Esther Rubens.
GUARD (*rising, opening the door* R. *and calling*). Miss Esther Rubens.

(ESTHER RUBENS *enters* R. *and crosses to the witness stand. She is a country girl wearing a checkered gingham frock, and a kerchief on her hair.*)

PROSECUTOR. Please take the stand.

(*After being sworn,* ESTHER *sits. The* GUARD *closes the door and sits.*)

What is your occupation, Miss Rubens?
ESTHER (*softly*). I am a farm hand.
PROSECUTOR. For whom do you work?
ESTHER (*softly*). Mr Jacobson hired me for the spring work in the garden.
PROSECUTOR. Speak up, my dear, so that the Jury can hear you. Don't be afraid.
ESTHER (*in a louder voice*). Mr Jacobson hired me for the spring work in the garden.
PROSECUTOR. Where did you spend the night of April eighth?
ESTHER. In the stable. That's where I sleep. I share it with the mule.
PROSECUTOR. I see. (*He pauses.*) Well, Miss Rubens, tell us what happened that night.
ESTHER. I went to sleep early, but just before morning, something woke me—a man was in the stable.
PROSECUTOR. Who was he?
ESTHER. I couldn't make out in the dark. I was afraid it was a soldier and I hid in the straw. You know, there were soldiers in the garden—they were there to watch the tomb. It was a cold night. . . .
PROSECUTOR. And you thought that perhaps a soldier wanted a little warming up.

(ESTHER *looks down.*)

(*After a pause. With a smile.*) Never mind, Miss Rubens. What did the man do?
ESTHER. He talked to the mule.

PROSECUTOR. Did you recognize the voice?

ESTHER. Yes—it was the gardener's. He took the mule out of the stable.

PROSECUTOR. Wasn't it rather unusual at that hour?

COUNSELLOR (*rising*). Objection!

JUDGE. Objection sustained.

(*The* COUNSELLOR *sits.*)

PROSECUTOR. I'll put the question another way. (*To* ESTHER.) Did such a thing ever happen before?

ESTHER. Not that I remember.

PROSECUTOR. Did he tell you where he was taking the mule?

ESTHER. He didn't talk to me. He thought I was asleep. But he must have hitched the mule to the water pump—I heard the wheel begin to squeak.

PROSECUTOR. What else did you hear?

ESTHER. Nothing else. It was pretty quiet for a while—but when morning came, I heard voices in the garden. I looked out and saw some city ladies. They came to see the grave—and were all excited because the tomb was open.

PROSECUTOR. How many women were there?

ESTHER. I'm not sure. Three or four—I guess it was four.

(*The* PROSECUTOR *moves down* c.)

Three of them went to the tomb, and one—she had red hair—ran back to the city.

PROSECUTOR. Red hair?

ESTHER (*animatedly*). Yes, sir. The other women shouted after her, "Where are you running, Magdalen?" But she was out of her mind, she just ran and kept screaming.

PROSECUTOR. Could you make out her cries?

ESTHER. She kept repeating the same thing. "The Master's body is stolen!"

PROSECUTOR. Are you sure she said—stolen?

ESTHER. Yes, sir.

PROSECUTOR. She didn't use the expression—risen?

COUNSELLOR (*rising*). Objection! The witness is not here to testify about an expression which was not used.

JUDGE. Objection sustained.

(*The* COUNSELLOR *sits.*)

PROSECUTOR (*to* ESTHER). And where was the gardener all this time, Miss Rubens?

ESTHER. He had come back to the stable with the mule.

PROSECUTOR. What was he doing?

ESTHER. He was all out of breath—and was cleaning fresh dirt from his shovel.

PROSECUTOR. Fresh dirt?

ESTHER. Yes, sir. I asked what he'd been digging.

PROSECUTOR. What did he answer?

ESTHER. He said he was trying to catch a mole. So I said that it was pretty dark yet to catch moles.

PROSECUTOR. And?

ESTHER. He told me to mind my own business. So I said to him, "You weren't out after a mole. You were digging a bigger hole than that."

PROSECUTOR (*satisfied*). That will be all, Miss Rubens. (*He moves to his chair down L. and sits.*) Your witness, Counsellor.

(*The* COUNSELLOR *rises.*)

COUNSELLOR. About that shovel, Miss Rubens. Are you sure there was fresh dirt on it?

ESTHER. Yes, sir.

COUNSELLOR (*looking steadily at* ESTHER). But you did not actually see the gardener digging?

ESTHER (*after a pause*). No, sir.

COUNSELLOR. Thank you, Miss Rubens. No more questions. (*He sits.*)

(ESTHER *rises, moves to the door L. and exits. The* PROSECUTOR *rises and calls the next witness.*)

PROSECUTOR. Private Sextus Lucius.

GUARD (*rising, opening the door R. and calling*). Private Sextus Lucius.

(PRIVATE LUCIUS *enters R. and crosses to the witness stand. In his field uniform he looks like a G.I. Only the shape of his helmet and the Roman insignia on his sleeve, a fasces with the lettering S.P.Q.R. reveal that he is a Roman soldier. After being sworn, he sits. The* GUARD *closes the door.*)

PROSECUTOR (*perching himself on the up R. corner of his table*). Private Lucius, do you remember the night of April eighth?

LUCIUS. Yes, sir.

PROSECUTOR. What were you doing that night?

LUCIUS. I was on guard duty before a tomb in a garden.

PROSECUTOR. What time did your watch begin?

LUCIUS. Midnight.

PROSECUTOR. At that time, was the stone over the tomb still in place?

LUCIUS. Yes, sir.

PROSECUTOR. And the body was inside?

LUCIUS. Must have been—the tomb was sealed.

PROSECUTOR. Did you know who the dead man was?

COUNSELLOR (*rising*). Objection! The charge is body-snatching The identity of the dead man is irrelevant.

PROSECUTOR (*rising; to the* JUDGE). Your Honour, in this case the identity is the motivation itself.

COUNSELLOR (*turning to the audience; sarcastically*). I take it for granted that the Jury knows who Jesus of Nazareth was.

JUDGE. The Jury is not to be influenced by any previous knowledge. Only evidence produced at this trial is to be considered. The Court permits the question.

(*The* COUNSELLOR *sits.*)

PROSECUTOR (*to* LUCIUS). Well, Private Lucius (*he moves* C.) did you know the man in the tomb?

LUCIUS. Yes, sir. He was one of the three that was put on the cross the other day—the fellow in the middle I guess.

PROSECUTOR. Is that the only thing you remember about him?

LUCIUS. He was sort of a skinny man.

PROSECUTOR (*emphatically*). A man—nothing but a man!

COUNSELLOR (*rising*). Objection!

JUDGE. Sustained!

(*The* COUNSELLOR *sits.*)

PROSECUTOR. What I mean is—was he any different from the others?

LUCIUS (*shrugging his shoulders*). They all look alike on the cross.

PROSECUTOR. You never saw him before?

LUCIUS. Once, in the Governor's court—when he was sentenced.

PROSECUTOR. Do you know why he was sentenced?

LUCIUS. No—I wasn't interested. Anyway, the whole thing didn't make sense to me. Just a lot of screaming and noise. Some sort of demonstration—the mob had it in for him.

PROSECUTOR (*moving and perching himself on his table*). I see. Well, Private Lucius, let's get back to what happened during your watch.

LUCIUS. I just stood there—hating every minute of it. What was I doing there—strange country, strange grave—what business was it of mine? It was a cold night and I . . . (*He hesitates.*)

PROSECUTOR. Go ahead, soldier, speak up.

LUCIUS. I was scared.

PROSECUTOR. An armed trooper—scared?

LUCIUS. I'm not afraid of anything living.

PROSECUTOR (*rising*). Surely you weren't frightened by a dead man?

LUCIUS. No. I've seen lots of them—some I knocked off myself. But I never had to stand watch over them at midnight. That gave me the creeps. I was plenty glad to hear footsteps.

PROSECUTOR (*breaking to* C.). Whose were they?

LUCIUS. The gardener's.

PROSECUTOR. Oh, the gardener! Do you see him in this room?

LUCIUS. Yes, sir.

PROSECUTOR. Will you point him out for us?
LUCIUS (*pointing to the* GARDENER). There he is.
PROSECUTOR. Thank you. What did he want?
LUCIUS. He brought me a pitcher of wine. Said it would take away the chill. (*He grins.*) It did.
PROSECUTOR. What happened then?
LUCIUS (*after a pause; embarrassed*). I fell asleep.
PROSECUTOR. Fell asleep—on guard duty. Was the wine drugged, do you think?
COUNSELLOR (*rising*). Objection!
JUDGE. Sustained!

(*The* COUNSELLOR *sits.*)

PROSECUTOR. How soon after drinking the wine did you fall asleep?
LUCIUS. It wasn't very long.
PROSECUTOR. And when did you awake?
LUCIUS. Just before it got light. There was a rumble. I jumped up and saw that the stone was pushed aside. The tomb was empty.
PROSECUTOR. And when you saw that?
LUCIUS. I took off to report that the body was stolen.
PROSECUTOR. That will be all, Private Lucius. (*He moves to his chair down* L. *and sits.*) Your witness, Counsellor.

(*The* COUNSELLOR *rises and moves* R.C.)

COUNSELLOR. You testified, Private Lucius, that the wine warmed you up.
LUCIUS. Yes, sir.
COUNSELLOR. Was it a strong wine?
LUCIUS. Sure was.
COUNSELLOR. How much of it did you drink?
LUCIUS. I took a pretty big swallow.
COUNSELLOR. Did you leave anything in the pitcher?
LUCIUS (*sheepishly*). Not much, I guess.
COUNSELLOR (*after a pause*). When you awoke, the stone was already rolled away?
LUCIUS. Yes, sir.
COUNSELLOR. Was the gardener around?
LUCIUS. No, sir.
COUNSELLOR. Did you make sure the tomb was empty?
LUCIUS. Yes, sir. I poked my head in.
COUNSELLOR. Wasn't it dark inside?
LUCIUS. Yes. It was pitch black.
COUNSELLOR. Then there might have been someone in there?
LUCIUS (*hesitantly*). Well—I did see something white.
COUNSELLOR (*tensely*). A man in a white robe?

Lucius. For a second that's what I thought—but then I saw that it was only a sheet and a napkin.

Counsellor. Oh—the burial cloths. (*He moves down* l.c.) Describe them to us. Were they rumpled?

Lucius. No, sir. The sheet was neatly folded and the napkin rolled up.

Counsellor (*to the audience*). Would a grave robber take time to do this?

Lucius. How would I know what the grave robber did? I was asleep.

Counsellor (*sharply*). If you were asleep, how could you know that the body was stolen?

Lucius. It didn't walk away.

Counsellor. That isn't for you to decide.

Prosecutor (*interjecting*). Dead men don't walk.

Judge. The State will wait to be recognized.

Prosecutor (*rising*). Sorry, Your Honour. (*He sits.*)

Counsellor (*moving up* c.). About your report, Private Lucius —exactly what did you say? Try to repeat it word for word.

Lucius. I don't remember exactly. I just said that the disciples stole the body.

Counsellor (*quickly*). *Disciples!* Who put that word in your mouth?

Prosecutor (*rising*). Objection! The Defence is implying that the witness was coached.

Counsellor (*to the* Judge). Your Honour, the witness is a simple soldier from a foreign country. His testimony proves complete ignorance of the happenings around him. He saw Jesus before Pilate. He saw him on the cross—and he had not the slightest idea of what it was all about. Now, suddenly, he speaks of disciples—a word obviously not his own. And the State is using *this* man as an important witness.

Judge. The value of the testimony will be determined by the Jury. Objection sustained.

(*The* Prosecutor *sits.*)

Counsellor (*to* Lucius). To get back to your report, Private Lucius—to whom did you make it?

Lucius. The High Priest.

Counsellor (*after a pause*). Is he your superior officer?

Lucius. No, sir.

Counsellor. A soldier is required to report directly to his superior in command. Who made it worth your while to make your report to the High Priest?

Prosecutor (*rising*). Objection!

Judge. Sustained!

(*The* Prosecutor *sits.*

COUNSELLOR (*moving in close to* R. *of the witness stand*). What is the penalty for a soldier who falls asleep on guard duty?

LUCIUS (*after a pause; in a low voice*). Death.

COUNSELLOR. Apparently you were not penalized. (*He gives* LUCIUS *a scrutinizing glance.*) Who interceded on your behalf?

LUCIUS. I don't know.

COUNSELLOR. Did the High Priest guarantee your safety provided you made a report that the disciples had stolen the body?

PROSECUTOR (*rising; vehemently*). Don't answer that. (*To the* JUDGE.) I object, Your Honour. The witness is not on trial.

JUDGE. Objection sustained.

(*The* PROSECUTOR *sits.*)

COUNSELLOR. No more questions. (*He moves to his chair down* R. *and sits.*)

(LUCIUS *rises, moves to the door* L. *and exits. The* PROSECUTOR *rises and calls the next witness.*)

PROSECUTOR. Mr Nathaniel Pinchas.

GUARD (*rising, opening the door* R. *and calling*). Mr Nathaniel Pinchas.

(MR PINCHAS *enters* R. *and crosses to the witness stand. He is a friendly little man, agile and obsequious.*)

PROSECUTOR. Will you take the stand, please.

(*After being sworn*, MR PINCHAS *sits. The* GUARD *closes the door and sits.*)

(*He moves to* R. *of his table.*) What is your occupation, Mr Pinchas?

PINCHAS. I have a draper's shop in Temple Square. We are a very well established firm. Nathaniel Pinchas and Sons. Silks, velvets, homespuns, hand-loomed linens—all kinds of textiles and finery.

PROSECUTOR (*moving* C.). The burial cloths found in the tomb— were they purchased in your shop?

PINCHAS. Yes, sir. On a Friday, a gentleman came into my shop with a friend. A very high-born gentleman, well-tailored, wealthy looking. He purchased a napkin of the finest fabric— and linen sheeting of the best quality. You know, sir, I carry only the best.

PROSECUTOR. I am sure of it. Did he say what the sheet was for?

PINCHAS. No, sir. But while I was cutting the linen in the back room, I heard the two gentlemen talking—and I gathered it was for a shroud. They also said something about moving the body in a couple of days.

PROSECUTOR (*moving to the witness stand; quickly*). A couple of days!

PINCHAS. Yes, sir.

PROSECUTOR. A couple of days from Friday would be Sunday.

PINCHAS. Yes, sir.

PROSECUTOR. So you can testify that they already knew **on** Friday that the body would be moved on Sunday.

COUNSELLOR (*rising*). I object! The question is leading.

JUDGE. Objection sustained.

(*The* COUNSELLOR *sits.*)

PROSECUTOR. Let me ask it another way. Are you positive that the conversation took place on Friday?

PINCHAS. Yes, sir. It was late afternoon, and the gentleman said he had to hurry before the Sabbath caught up with him.

PROSECUTOR. And how did he pay you? Cash?

PINCHAS. No, sir. He was a gentleman—he charged it.

PROSECUTOR. What was his name?

PINCHAS. Joseph of Arimathea. And good enough for me. (*Respectfully.*) A Senator—the head of the biggest law office. . . .

PROSECUTOR. A very good account indeed, Mr Pinchas. That will do. (*He moves to his chair and sits.*) Your witness, Counsellor.

COUNSELLOR. No questions.

(PINCHAS *rises, moves to the door* L. *and exits. The* PROSECUTOR *rises and calls the next witness.*)

PROSECUTOR. Mr Joseph of Arimathea.

GUARD (*rising; opening the door* R. *and calling*). Mr Joseph of Arimathea.

(JOSEPH OF ARIMATHEA *enters* R. *and crosses to the witness stand. In his dark blue suit and conservative necktie, he looks just as he had been described—distinguished, well-tailored, wealthy.*)

PROSECUTOR. Please take the stand.

(*After being sworn,* JOSEPH *sits. The* GUARD *closes the door and sits.*)

(*He breaks to* C.) Mr Arimathea, it was testified that you are an attorney-at-law and a member of the Senate.

JOSEPH. Also an investment broker.

PROSECUTOR. You appear to have various interests.

JOSEPH. It is written in the scriptures that besides studying the law a man should have a trade.

PROSECUTOR (*easing* L.C.). You also have excellent connections.

JOSEPH. My friends are very kind. . . .

PROSECUTOR. And helpful. Governor Pilate released the body of Jesus of Nazareth to you?

JOSEPH. Yes, sir. After he died on the cross, I asked permission to make the final arrangements.

PROSECUTOR (*moving in to the witness stand*). He was taken down in an unusually short time. Did Jesus *really* die on the cross?

COUNSELLOR (*rising quickly*). The charge is body-snatching.

That assumes the existence of a dead body. Does the Prosecutor question the validity of his own indictment? Or is he just using this trial to discredit what we know to be the truth—that Jesus is risen?

PROSECUTOR (*breaking* R.C. *and facing the* COUNSELLOR). If the Counsellor doubts the validity of the indictment, why doesn't he make a motion to dismiss? Or is he just using this trial to substantiate what we know to be a hoax—entitled—resurrection?

JUDGE. The gentlemen will refrain from exchanging personal opinions and recriminations. The Jury will disregard all statements made by opposing counsel regarding each other's motives.

PROSECUTOR. I withdraw the question.

(*The* COUNSELLOR *sits.*)

(*After a pause. To* JOSEPH.) Why did you claim the body from Governor Pilate?

JOSEPH. For strictly personal reasons.

PROSECUTOR (*moving* C.). Did someone support you in this request?

JOSEPH. Yes, sir.

PROSECUTOR. Who was it?

JOSEPH (*after a pause*). I'd rather not involve anyone.

PROSECUTOR. I must insist. Was it a lady?

JOSEPH. It was.

PROSECUTOR. A high-ranking lady?

JOSEPH (*snobbishly*). I don't know any other kind.

PROSECUTOR. Was she the wife of Governor Pilate?

JOSEPH. If I must answer—yes.

PROSECUTOR. Why did you ask for her support?

JOSEPH. I was aware of her sympathy towards Jesus and I knew she would help.

PROSECUTOR. Are you a follower of Jesus of Nazareth?

JOSEPH (*after a pause; uncertainly*). Well—that's not so easy to answer.

PROSECUTOR. Answer yes or no.

JOSEPH. Sir, I am a Senator—I have to consider any statement I make.

PROSECUTOR. But you must know where you stand.

JOSEPH (*with dignity*). As a member of the investigating Committee, it is my duty to analyse all political, spiritual and religious movements in Palestine. That's how I first learned of Jesus and became attracted to his teachings.

PROSECUTOR. May I inquire what was attractive about them?

JOSEPH. Originally, his stand on the income tax question. He said you may serve God and still pay taxes to Caesar. I found it a sensible solution. The only way for the Jew to survive under the Roman.

PROSECUTOR (*breaking down* C.). Then you considered him from a financial point of view?

JOSEPH. Only before I met him. After that, it was the man himself who intrigued me—his strange charm.

PROSECUTOR. Charm?

JOSEPH. I know, it's a peculiar way to describe him—but he was charming—so much so that people gave up their business to follow him.

PROSECUTOR (*moving down* L.). What business did *you* give up, Senator?

JOSEPH. I'm not an impulsive man. But he disturbed me—he made me wonder about many things.

PROSECUTOR. How did you meet him?

JOSEPH. At a dinner-party—in the house of a mutual friend. Strangely enough, at first I considered him provincial. He used rather simple language. I might even say he spoke in agricultural terms. Wheat, grapes—bread and wine. Then suddenly it occurred to me that that's what truth really is—basic, simple, clean—like bread and wine.

PROSECUTOR. So that was your reason for claiming his body from Pilate.

JOSEPH. I felt I owed him a funeral. (*Humbly.*) He gave me the words of life—I gave him a shroud and a grave.

PROSECUTOR (*moving in to the witness stand; sharply*). In your garden! Where you had complete control over his body.

JOSEPH. Control?

PROSECUTOR. You could have it moved at your will.

JOSEPH. If I chose.

PROSECUTOR. A most convenient location for staging a miracle.

COUNSELLOR (*rising*). Objection!

JUDGE. Sustained!

(*The* COUNSELLOR *sits.*)

PROSECUTOR (*to* JOSEPH). You knew the body would be moved, even before you buried it?

JOSEPH. That is correct, sir.

PROSECUTOR. And you gave the gardener orders to dig a grave?

JOSEPH. I did.

PROSECUTOR. No more questions. (*He moves to his chair down* L. *and sits.*) Your witness, Counsellor.

(*The* COUNSELLOR *rises and moves* C.)

COUNSELLOR. You are a wealthy man, Senator Arimathea?

JOSEPH (*after a pause*). God has favoured me. Particularly in export—import.

COUNSELLOR. I understand you also have large real estate holdings.

PROSECUTOR (*rising*). Objection! Immaterial.

B

JUDGE. What purpose has the Defence in asking these questions?

COUNSELLOR (*to the* JUDGE). To counter, Your Honour, the inference that Senator Arimathea would in any way involve himself in the crime alleged by the State. He is a citizen of standing and integrity. He is a rich man. And rich men are afraid of changes. It would be against his whole background and tradition to fake a miracle—a miracle bound to change the destiny of the world.

JUDGE. In principle, the Court will permit questions concerning character and background. Objection overruled.

(*The* PROSECUTOR *sits.*)

COUNSELLOR (*moving in to* R. *of* JOSEPH). Are you friendly with Governor Pilate, Senator?

JOSEPH. We're on fairly intimate terms.

COUNSELLOR. Did he release the body to you readily?

JOSEPH. He made no objections.

COUNSELLOR. Was it because he had confidence in you?

JOSEPH. I believe so.

COUNSELLOR (*after a pause*). Why did you plan to move the body from the tomb?

JOSEPH. The tomb was intended only as a temporary resting place until the Sabbath was over.

COUNSELLOR. Was the tomb guarded at all times?

JOSEPH. Night and day.

COUNSELLOR. And the stone before the entrance—was it a heavy one?

JOSEPH. Exceedingly heavy.

COUNSELLOR. Could it be moved by human power?

PROSECUTOR (*rising*). Objection! The stone was set there by human power—consequently, it could have been removed by human power.

JUDGE. Objection sustained.

(*The* PROSECUTOR *sits.*)

COUNSELLOR. Senator Arimathea, did *you* roll away the stone?

JOSEPH. No, sir.

COUNSELLOR. Did you hire anyone to roll it away?

JOSEPH. No, sir.

COUNSELLOR. Did you have anything whatsoever to do with the disappearance of the body from the tomb?

JOSEPH. No, sir.

COUNSELLOR. Thank you, Senator. That's all. (*He moves to his chair down* R. *and sits.*)

(JOSEPH *rises and moves to the door* L. *The* PROSECUTOR *rises and calls the next witness.*)

PROSECUTOR. Lady Procula Claudia.

GUARD (*rising, opening the door* R. *and calling*). Lady Procula Claudia.

(LADY PROCULA *enters* R., *and crosses to the witness stand.* JOSEPH *bows to her, then turns and exits* L. LADY PROCULA *is a socialite in her forties, and she manages to look very attractive in a smart frock and a brand new Easter bonnet.*)

PROSECUTOR. Will you please take the stand.

(*After being sworn,* LADY PROCULA *sits and lifts her veil. The* GUARD *closes the door and sits.*)

(*He moves* C.) Lady Procula—you are the wife of Governor Pontius Pilate?

PROCULA. I am.

PROSECUTOR. And as his wife, you have some word in matters of administration?

PROCULA. Not as a rule. My duties are mostly social and extremely trying. I have to divide my time between Caesarea and Jerusalem. We have two households, two sets of friends, double chance to make enemies—if you know what I mean.

PROSECUTOR (*smiling*). You have all my sympathies, Lady Procula.

PROCULA. My position is very delicate. We are conquerors, and people are sensitive. Every dinner is a major problem. Whom to invite with whom—seeing to it that the right persons are on the right couches. . . .

PROSECUTOR. I beg your pardon. . . .

PROCULA. We Romans take our meals in comfort, reclining at our ease.

PROSECUTOR. Of course. So as I understand it, you keep yourself remote from actual political events.

PROCULA. As far as possible.

PROSECUTOR. But you did interfere in the case of Jesus of Nazareth.

PROCULA. Definitely. I liked the man.

PROSECUTOR. Did you ever meet him?

PROCULA (*casually*). Oh, yes. My husband was away in Rome and I was invited for a weekend. It was at a ranch in Bethany, close to Jerusalem. We were just about to break up when he dropped in.

PROSECUTOR. And you stayed on?

PROCULA. We all did. He came with an interesting assortment of people, mostly fishermen—colourful characters. We all sat under an olive tree and he talked. He was quite a raconteur. I recall one of his stories about some girls who were waiting for the bridegroom, and when he arrived they had no oil in their lamps. I didn't quite get the point, but he was fascinating to listen to. He was so utterly different.

PROSECUTOR. In what way?

PROCULA. How can I explain it? I couldn't classify him. He was far from the athletic type so over-rated by Roman women. But he wasn't the kind of sophisticated man who can make life so disappointing. He wasn't smooth like a Greek, yet he wasn't clumsy like a barbarian. I wouldn't call him aristocratic, but he certainly wasn't common. He was very informal, but still he had some humble dignity. He had the most impressive eyes. He must have been a wonderful physician.

PROSECUTOR (*surprised*). Physician?

PROCULA. That's what I heard he was. He healed so many people. . . .

PROSECUTOR (*cutting her short*). Tell us, Lady Procula, (*he moves down* L.) when did you meet him next?

PROCULA (*with a little sigh*). Never—but I thought of him a lot —I even dreamt about him. Isn't it odd! The very day after my dream he was arrested.

PROSECUTOR. You tried to save him?

PROCULA. I did everything. But it was just one of those ghastly situations where nothing could be done. My husband was in a difficult situation—so all I could do was to turn to Rufio.

PROSECUTOR. Who is Rufio?

(*There is a pause.*)

PROCULA. Oh—the Captain who escorted Jesus to the cross. (*She pauses.*) I gave him a bottle of wine and asked him to give some to Jesus. It was very strong wine—I thought it would dull his pain. But he refused the wine. What magnificent spirit! The Captain came back deeply shaken. . . .

PROSECUTOR (*interrupting sharply*). Was this the same Captain who had charge of the guard before the tomb?

PROCULA. I believe he was.

PROSECUTOR. And did you, by any chance, suggest to him that the sentries look the other way when the disciples came for the body?

PROCULA (*with a shade of disappointment*). Did they really come for the body? It was such a comfort to believe that he returned from the dead. You know, I wasn't at all surprised when I heard he had. I had a strange feeling he couldn't have gone forever.

PROSECUTOR (*moving* C.; *nervously*). You cannot be serious, Lady Procula!

PROCULA (*argumentatively*). Why? It wouldn't be the first time such a thing has happened. Didn't Orpheus come back from Hades with the help of a faithful woman?

PROSECUTOR (*moving to* PROCULA; *cutting her short*). Let's not discuss old love stories. (*Abruptly.*) Thank you, Lady Procula. I have no more questions. (*He moves to his chair down* L. *and sits.*) Your witness, Counsellor.

(*The* Counsellor *rises and moves* c. *with a gratified air.*)

Counsellor. Your testimony, Lady Procula, revealed a quality of faith.

Procula. You mean—I am credulous. I was driven to it by sheer boredom. Palestine is a dull place. No theatres, no concerts —minor league sports. In desperation I began to think—but I soon stopped.

Counsellor. May I ask why?

Procula. I was in danger of becoming profound—and depths frighten me. So I just satisfied myself with a glimpse into the infinite.

Counsellor. Then you admit he was infinite?

Prosecutor (*rising*). Objection!

Judge. Sustained.

(*The* Prosecutor *sits.*)

Counsellor (*breaking down* c.). Lady Procula, as wife of the Governor, you had an inside view of all these events?

Procula. I did.

Counsellor (*after a pause*). Had you any knowledge of a conspiracy to steal the body?

Procula. None whatsoever.

Counsellor (*after a pause*). Are you a Christian, Lady Procula?

Procula (*hesitantly*). I don't know—but as I said, I like the man.

Counsellor. Then you *are* a Christian. (*He gives her a polite bow.*) Thank you. (*He moves to his chair down* R. *and sits.*)

(Lady Procula *rises, moves to the door* L. *and exits. The* Prosecutor *rises, and with a certain deference, calls the next witness.*)

Prosecutor. His Excellency, Governor Pontius Pilate.

Guard (*rising, opening the door* R. *and calling*). His Excellency, Governor Pontius Pilate.

(Pilate *enters, moves* c., *and bows to the* Judge. *He is dressed in a white tropical suit after the fashion of British officials in Africa and the Orient. Though a Roman, the fact that he represents a Colonial Empire gives him something that we today call, a British air. This does not mean he is corpulent like Winston Churchill, or slender and welltailored like Anthony Eden. He is a blend of the two. He has taken on some weight during his long service, but in his younger days he must have been handsome.*)

Prosecutor. Will you please take the stand.

(Pilate *moves to the witness stand, and after being sworn, sits and attentively waits for the questions. The* Guard *closes the door and sits.*)

(*He moves* c.) You are the Governor of Judea, Your Excellency?

PILATE. Unfortunately! I have the privilege of representing Caesar in the most troublesome spot in our Commonwealth.

PROSECUTOR. Troublesome? Are you referring to the case we are trying here?

PILATE. The Nazarene? Oh, no. He was only an incident among the various annoyances in my administration.

PROSECUTOR (*respectfully*). Won't you please tell the Jury about this incident, Governor?

PILATE. As much as I can recall. The first day of Passover, a man was delivered to me by the local government. They asked for a sentence of death. I regarded the whole thing with the utmost suspicion.

PROSECUTOR. Did you have any special reason for this?

PILATE. No—it was part of a general suspicion. (*With a note of anger.*) From the moment I took office I constantly had the feeling of being out-smarted.

PROSECUTOR. By whom?

PILATE. A God—the Jewish God.

PROSECUTOR. Will you kindly explain that.

PILATE. We have encountered many Gods in many countries protected by the arm of Rome. Gods of gold, of jade or ivory. Some gods had pot-bellies and two heads. I've met divine bulls, sacred cows, holy cats. But they were all visible. We could liquidate them if they refused to co-operate. The Jewish God was different. He was invisible. You cannot liquidate the invisible.

PROSECUTOR (*moving to* PILATE). In what way did this influence your attitude towards Jesus of Nazareth?

PILATE. It was the very reason for my interest in him. The visible son of an invisible God! At last, here was something I could take hold of. With his son in my power, we could force the Jewish God to make a deal with the Romans.

PROSECUTOR (*smiling*). But you soon discovered he wasn't the son of God.

COUNSELLOR (*rising*). Objection!

JUDGE. Sustained!

(*The* COUNSELLOR *sits.*)

PROSECUTOR. Did you ever discover who he was, Excellency?

PILATE. Eh?

PROSECUTOR. Did you ever discover who he was, Excellency?

PILATE. It was never quite clear to me. A carpenter—a King—a prophet—or just a Jew with a new proposition.

PROSECUTOR. After his death, Excellency, did *you* order the watch at the tomb?

PILATE. Yes.

PROSECUTOR (*moving down* L.). Was it an established custom to post a watch over bodies of executed men?

PILATE. No. As a matter of fact, I'm afraid I created a precedent.

PROSECUTOR. Why did you do it?

PILATE. I acceded to a request of the High Priest. He called upon me personally and expressed concern that the Disciples would steal their Master's body. He produced reports from his Secret Service. The Nazarene had made some kind of statement about rising on the third day—and his disciples didn't want to make a liar out of him. We had to prevent the creation of a legend.

PROSECUTOR. Were you afraid of legends?

PILATE. The city was restless. And this kind of legend was dangerous. It promised the masses intervention by a higher power. It raised doubt where real authority lay. (*Arbitrarily.*) As a Roman Governor I couldn't tolerate this. I decided to seal the tomb and put a guard before it.

PROSECUTOR. In anticipation of an attempt to rob the grave?

PILATE. Yes. If they removed the statue of Caesar—certainly they would not stop at the body of a Jew.

PROSECUTOR. No, they would not.

COUNSELLOR (*rising*). Objection!

JUDGE. Sustained!

(*The* COUNSELLOR *sits.*)

PROSECUTOR. That's all, Excellency. Thank you very much. (*He moves to his chair down* L. *and sits.*) Your witness, Counsellor.

(*The* COUNSELLOR *rises and moves* C.)

COUNSELLOR. About that alleged conspiracy, Your Excellency —did you order an investigation of your own?

PILATE. No. I considered it a strictly internal affair.

COUNSELLOR. Then you relied upon information supplied by a prejudiced party—I might say a very prejudiced party.

PILATE. Our policy was to give local authorities the widest possible latitude.

COUNSELLOR. Without taking pains to establish the truth?

PILATE. My long years of public service have made me somewhat sceptical about truth. I've found that truth is a question of geography. In one place, they put you on a pedestal—the other, on the gallows.

COUNSELLOR (*after a pause*). You put him on the gallows.

PILATE. The time demanded it. He came when truth was out of season.

COUNSELLOR (*after a pause; breaking down* C.). So you simply accepted as a fact that someone had stolen the body?

PILATE. It was common sense. My seal on the tomb was broken.

COUNSELLOR (*after a pause; moving to* PILATE). Maybe it was Jesus who broke it.

PILATE. You can't ask a Roman to believe that.

COUNSELLOR. But you do believe in some God?

PILATE. Eh?

COUNSELLOR. But you do believe in some God?

PILATE. I am looking for one. There's a great shortage of Gods. We have to use substitutes—philosophy—synthetic Gods. But they don't last long. A God should last for ever.

COUNSELLOR (*moving down* L.). How very true!

PILATE (*wistfully*). If only the Jews would share with us the secret of their God—we Romans could develop him to perfection. That's our greatness. Improving on original ideas.

COUNSELLOR. You sound cynical, Pilate. But you are not. You show definite signs of sympathy towards Jesus of Nazareth.

PILATE. I found no crime in this man. In fact, I wanted to use him.

COUNSELLOR. For what purpose?

PILATE. I heard he could cure an aching back with a touch of his hand. But unfortunately, some of his statements could be interpreted as a challenge to the omnipotence of Caesar. And that settled it. I couldn't save him. It wasn't personal. Strictly politics.

COUNSELLOR (*after a pause*). Is that an apology?

PILATE. Indeed, sir, it is. Politics! Serving the highest principles with the lowest methods. The High Priest threatened to report him to Rome as a menace to the lifeline of the Empire. My position was endangered.

COUNSELLOR (*after a pause*). Therefore, you sentenced him to death.

PILATE. It was the quickest way to put an end to this unpleasant episode.

COUNSELLOR (*moving* C.; *sarcastically*). Very far-sighted statesmanship.

PILATE (*taking the remark as a compliment*). In proportion to the issues involved, he wasn't important. Just another Jew. One more or less, I thought, would hardly make any difference.

COUNSELLOR (*smiling pensively*). This one made all the difference in the world. (*He moves to his chair down* R.) No more questions. (*He sits.*)

(PILATE *rises and moves to the door* L. *The* PROSECUTOR *rises and calls the next witness.*)

PROSECUTOR. Mr Saul, please.

GUARD (*rising, opening the door* R. *and calling*). Mr Saul.

(SAUL *enters* R. *and crosses to the witness stand. There is a sharp contrast between* PILATE *in his white tropical attire, and* SAUL *in his shapeless black suit. Though he wears a clerical collar, there is very little of the ecclesiastic about him—more of the businessman preoccupied in a very serious project. Massive and austere, he has strong features, deep charcoal eyes under bushy brows, and a determined chin underlined by dark whiskers. He walks towards the stand with a sort of awkward steadi-*

ness. His heavy boots with their thick soles, show signs of long and weary travel along dusty roads.)

PROSECUTOR. Mr Saul of Tarsus, take the stand.

(After being sworn, SAUL sits. The GUARD closes the door and sits. PILATE exits L.)

(He perches himself on the R. edge of his table.) Mr Tarsus, during that particular Passover, were you in Jerusalem?

SAUL. Yes, sir. I was.

PROSECUTOR. Are you a permanent resident there?

SAUL. No, sir. *(He smiles pensively.)* I never settle down.

PROSECUTOR. But you did spend many years there.

SAUL. I worked my way through college.

PROSECUTOR. As a salesman?

SAUL. Originally, I was a tent-maker. I was born in Tarsus of Cilicia. That's goat country, you know. They make the finest tents there.

PROSECUTOR. Tarsus—that's a Greek city.

SAUL. I am a Jew.

PROSECUTOR. With a Roman passport?

SAUL. The only way to travel—and I have to travel a great deal.

PROSECUTOR. What is your business?

SAUL. I am a Deputy of the great council of Jerusalem—in charge of inter-Jewish relations.

PROSECUTOR. What does that mean?

SAUL. Control over Jewish communities dispersed through Syria and Asia Minor. Far from the Holy City, they took liberties with the law. I had to bring them back to orthodoxy—to restore a strict dogma.

PROSECUTOR. And in the course of this mission, you had to deal with the teachings of Jesus?

SAUL. I immediately recognized the danger in him. I studied the matter thoroughly. I traced it back to its very source—the empty tomb.

PROSECUTOR. Then you are familiar with the case on trial.

SAUL. I know the facts.

PROSECUTOR *(rising and moving C.).* What are they? Will you please tell the Jury.

SAUL. The whole thing is a fake—a plot of clumsy Galilean fishermen.

PROSECUTOR. But aren't you a Pharisee?

SAUL. I am.

PROSECUTOR. Pharisees believe in the resurrection of the dead.

SAUL. We do.

PROSECUTOR. And still you don't believe that Jesus has risen?

SAUL. The dead will rise when the Messiah comes, and only then—at the end of time. He couldn't have risen.

PROSECUTOR. On what do you base this knowledge?

SAUL. Testimony and Bible.

PROSECUTOR. Aren't they one and the same?

SAUL. Not quite. Bible is testimony—but testimony is not Bible.

PROSECUTOR. Did you major in Bible study?

SAUL. I was a pupil of the greatest masters—I can recognize a false prophet when I see one.

PROSECUTOR (*breaking down* c.). Was Jesus a false prophet?

COUNSELLOR (*rising*). I object, Your Honour! The witness is here to give evidence of fact—and not conclusions of his own.

PROSECUTOR (*to the* JUDGE). If it please, Your Honour. Mr Saul of Tarsus is a qualified witness. The State must challenge the absurdity of the contention that a body got up one Sunday morning and walked out of its grave. The State desires to prove that Jesus was not endowed with powers for such a performance. So, we are simply making use of Mr Tarsus' expert knowledge of religious background. . . .

JUDGE (*rapping with his gavel; interrupting*). The witness has been qualified. Objection overruled.

(*The* COUNSELLOR *sits.*)

(*To* SAUL.) The witness may answer.

SAUL. The Nazarene was a false prophet. I can prove it with the Scriptures. As a matter of fact, I am on a lecture tour on the subject. As soon as the Court excuses me, I leave for Damascus.

PROSECUTOR. Damascus?

SAUL. That's my next stop.

PROSECUTOR. And what will you tell Damascus?

SAUL. What I tell every village and hamlet. He was a deceiver. He must be destroyed. . . .

COUNSELLOR (*interjecting*). By throwing stones at his disciples.

JUDGE (*rapping with his gavel*). Counsel for Defence is out of order.

COUNSELLOR (*rising*). I apologize, Your Honour. (*He sits.*)

PROSECUTOR (*breaking down* R.; *suavely*). I wish the Counsel to be entirely satisfied. (*To* SAUL.) Did you stone Stephen, Mr Tarsus?

SAUL. I never touched a stone. I fought with words. Well, these words put stones in the people's hands. They killed Stephen and taught me a great lesson. For the first time I saw the power of the word. If it could move stones, it could move mountains—if it could move mountains, it could move the world. More than that —it could create a world.

PROSECUTOR (*breaking* c.). And with the power of the word, Saul of Tarsus, do you testify that Jesus has not risen?

SAUL. I do.

PROSECUTOR. Thank you. (*He moves to his chair down* L. *and sits.*) Your witness, Counsellor.

(*The* COUNSELLOR *rises and moves* C.)

COUNSELLOR. Mr Saul of Tarsus, you just testified that the word can do everything.

SAUL. That's correct.

COUNSELLOR. Well, then, why cannot the word open a tomb?

SAUL. It can. It will open all tombs when the Christ comes. But Jesus was not the Christ.

COUNSELLOR (*sternly*). A strong statement, Saul of Tarsus.

SAUL. I have strong beliefs.

COUNSELLOR. You intend to destroy Jesus?

SAUL. I will!

COUNSELLOR. You persecute his disciples?

SAUL. I do!

COUNSELLOR. You want to exterminate them—to the last one?

SAUL. I hope to!

COUNSELLOR. By any means? Even by false testimony?

PROSECUTOR (*rising and moving to* L. *of the* COUNSELLOR; *emphatically*). I object, Your Honour!

(*The clash is so violent that there is a flurry of excitement in the courtroom*)

I object most strenuously! False testimony. . . .

JUDGE (*rapping with his gavel*). Objection sustained. Counsel will be careful not to prejudice the witness before the Jury. If he has any evidence to support his implication, he should introduce it by means of direct testimony.

(*The* PROSECUTOR *moves to his chair down* L. *and sits.*)

COUNSELLOR (*to* JUDGE). I withdraw the question, Your Honour. (*To* SAUL.) What proof do you have, Mr Tarsus, that he is not the Messiah?

SAUL. This very argument. When the real Messiah comes there will be no argument, no doubt, no misgiving. He will appear with terrifying simplicity. Knowledge and faith will be the same. Everyone will believe—the wise and the fool.

COUNSELLOR. Which are you, Saul of Tarsus?

SAUL. Neither—or both. God makes me what I am—Israel, chained to Him by His promise. Reeling under the weight of His love.

COUNSELLOR (*moving in to* R. *of* SAUL). Jesus came to ease your burden. Why did you refuse his help?

SAUL (*obstinately*). We aren't supposed to be helped. We cannot take the easy road. We cannot even help ourselves by calling the name of the Holy. The word can never be spoken. We guard it in eternal silence. We guard it with sealed lips. We guard it with the letter. We write it down, but never read it. We guard it by law.

Relentless, heavy, final. A comma cannot be changed. (*He rises. With suppressed rage.*) But he came from Nazareth and . . .

COUNSELLOR (*interrupting*). He might have changed some commas, but he didn't break the law.

(SAUL *resumes his seat.*)

SAUL (*after a pause*). He did worse. He relaxed it. (*Sternly.*) By breaking the law a Jew can only die—by relaxing it, he might become a Christian.

COUNSELLOR. And that's why you crucified him?

SAUL (*with great dignity*). I expected this accusation, Mr Counsellor, and I'll answer it with your own creed. Suppose he *was* the Christ you claim him to be. According to your teachings he had to be crucified—not by the Jew—not by the Roman—but by the will of his Father. We only would have assisted at his inauguration.

COUNSELLOR. I don't like that expression.

SAUL (*deliberating*). I am a man of public relations, sir. I know exactly what expressions to use. According to *your* teachings, Calvary *was* an inauguration to Heavenly Glory—and we had to assist against our will—confirming the very thing we deny. (*He pauses.*) We were nothing but a weapon chosen by the Father to kill His Son. (*He pauses.*) A weapon cannot be guilty. A tool cannot be blamed. (*He pauses.*) It's a tragic privilege to be the chosen one—and we should be respected for this, if your gospel is true. (*Very calmly.*) For I am not just a witness under cross-examination. I am neither a witness for the Defence, nor a witness for the State. (*He rises.*) I am a Jew—a witness for God.

COUNSELLOR. No more questions. (*He gives* SAUL *a long glance.*) I believe you have an appointment in Damascus. (*He moves to his chair down* R. *and sits.*)

(SAUL *rises and with determined mien, moves to the door* L. *and exits. The* PROSECUTOR *rises. There is a moment of silence. The lights start to dim out.*)

JUDGE (*rapping with his gavel*). The Court is adjourned until tomorrow at midnight.

The LIGHTS *Black-Out as—*

the CURTAIN *falls.*

ACT II

SCENE.—*The same. The following night.*

When the CURTAIN *rises, the stage is in darkness. After a moment the rapping of the gavel is heard and the lights come up. The* JUDGE, PROSECUTOR, COUNSELLOR, CLERK, GARDENER *and* GUARD *are seated in their places. The trial continues.*

JUDGE (*to the* PROSECUTOR). Has the State any other witnesses?
PROSECUTOR (*rising*). Yes, Your Honour. (*He calls the next witness.*) Miss Beulah Adams.
GUARD (*rising, opening the door* R. *and calling*). Miss Beulah Adams.

(BEULAH *enters* R. *and crosses to the witness stand. She is a pretty girl with very emphatic contours, and is healthy and supple. Her skin has the attractive shade of terra-cotta. She is very colourful in her flimsy something which we might call a print dress.*)

PROSECUTOR. Will you please take the stand.

(*After being sworn,* BEULAH *sits. The* GUARD *closes the door and sits.*)

(*He moves down* L. *of the witness stand.*) You're a barmaid, Miss Beulah?
BEULAH. Yes, Mr Prosecutor. I work at the *Three Cedars* Inn.
PROSECUTOR. *Three Cedars?* Where is that?
BEULAH. At the Damascus Gate. It's a hang-out for Roman soldiers.
PROSECUTOR. I suppose you know many of them.
BEULAH. Quite a few.
PROSECUTOR. By name?
BEULAH. Well, no—mostly I know them by their shoulder patches.
PROSECUTOR (*after a pause*). Tell us, Miss Beulah, do you remember the day Jesus was crucified?
BEULAH. Yes, Mr Prosecutor. It was on a Friday. I remember it was my day off. Just my luck!
PROSECUTOR. What do you mean by that?
BEULAH. I had a date with a soldier—but that night he was ordered to guard the tomb.
PROSECUTOR. And he didn't keep his date with you?
BEULAH. No, sir. But I went out to him. I got in the garden all right, but they wouldn't let me near him. No-one could approach the tomb. So I just stood there for a while and waited.

PROSECUTOR. All by yourself?

BEULAH. There were other visitors, too. Some women—waiting under the trees.

PROSECUTOR. How many women?

BEULAH. I'm not sure—five or six. They kept in the shadows.

PROSECUTOR. Can you describe them to us?

BEULAH. I remember only one. She stood out from the others. When a soldier threw kindling on the fire, I saw her face. She had big eyes and beautiful red hair.

PROSECUTOR (*quickly*). Red hair, did you say?

BEULAH. Yes, sir. I thought she'd come to meet a soldier, too. But she hadn't. She looked sad—just stood staring at the tomb— never took her eyes away for a minute.

PROSECUTOR (*urgently*). How long did this keep up? Did you hear them talking?

BEULAH. Just a few words. She said something about the stone —that the stone was very heavy—they'd need help to move it.

PROSECUTOR (*eagerly*). Move it!

BEULAH. Yes, sir.

PROSECUTOR (*moving down* C.). And didn't this strike you as somewhat strange?

BEULAH. I didn't think about it then—but I remembered it three days later when the body was stolen.

PROSECUTOR. How did you find out the body was stolen?

BEULAH. Sunday, when the soldiers got off guard duty, they came in to the *Three Cedars*. I waited on them and heard them talking. They were having a high old time—drinking and gambling. They played dice.

PROSECUTOR. For big stakes?

BEULAH. Very big! The money was piled up on the table. I got excited!

PROSECUTOR. Why? It wasn't your money.

BEULAH (*demurely*). No—but I was going to like the winner.

PROSECUTOR (*breaking to* R. *of* BEULAH; *smiling*). I see. (*He pauses.*) Well, Miss Beulah—is it usual for soldiers to have so much money?

BEULAH. Not as far as I know, Mr Prosecutor. Their whole year's pay wouldn't be as much as the money I saw on the table.

PROSECUTOR. And did they drop any hints where all this money came from?

BEULAH. When I asked them, they just winked, and said someone paid off for a little favour.

PROSECUTOR (*quickly*). A little favour! Do you suppose it was to look the other way when the disciples came to steal the body?

COUNSELLOR (*rising*). Objection!

JUDGE. Sustained!

(*The* COUNSELLOR *sits.*)

PROSECUTOR. Thanks, Beulah.

BEULAH. It's a pleasure, Prosecutor.

PROSECUTOR (*moving to his chair down* L.). Your witness, Counsellor. (*He sits.*)

(*The* COUNSELLOR *rises and moves* C.)

COUNSELLOR (*to the* JUDGE). On second thoughts, Your Honour, I withdraw my objection. My opponent has brought up the question of bribery. This bribe money might have come from another source than the State implied. (*To* BEULAH.) Miss Beulah—you stated that a mysterious someone gave the soldiers money—didn't you?

BEULAH. Yes, sir—I'm sure there was someone.

COUNSELLOR. Yes, there was—an interest that wanted to suppress the real fact—(*he moves down* R.)—that the body was never stolen!

PROSECUTOR (*rising*). Objection!

JUDGE. Sustained.

(*The* PROSECUTOR *sits.*)

COUNSELLOR (*moving to his chair down* R.). No more questions. (*He sits.*)

(BEULAH *rises and moves to the door* L. *The* PROSECUTOR *rises and calls the next witness.*)

PROSECUTOR. Mr Jesse Sadoc.

GUARD (*rising, opening the door* R. *and calling*). Mr Jesse Sadoc.

(MR JESSE SADOC *enters* R. *and crosses to the witness stand. He is of medium height with a wily face, alert eyes, and a very short neck. His head, bent to one side, seems to grow without a stem from his shoulders. Nevertheless, he is not a hunchback; just a man fixed in a permanent shrug.*)

PROSECUTOR. Will you take the stand, please.

BEULAH. Hiya, Jesse.

(*She exits* R. *After being sworn,* SADOC *sits. The* GUARD *closes the door and sits.*)

PROSECUTOR (*moving* C.). What is your profession, Mr Sadoc?

SADOC. I am a private detective.

PROSECUTOR. Then you'll understand why I ask you to face the Jury and answer all my questions to them.

SADOC. Yes, sir, I'll do just that.

PROSECUTOR (*easing down* C.; *with his back half turned to the audience*). Did you make an investigation of the disappearance of the body of Jesus of Nazareth?

SADOC. Yes, sir.

PROSECUTOR. Who hired you to do this?

SADOC. Interests close to the Government.

PROSECUTOR. Why were you chosen for this work?

SADOC. They knew I kept a complete file on Jesus and his disciples. I followed their every move for a long time.

PROSECUTOR. Did you have good sources of information?

SADOC. Good and reliable. One of his disciples was my half-brother. He kept his father's name—Iscariot.

PROSECUTOR (*after a pause*). Judas Iscariot is your half-brother!

SADOC. Yes, he was. But we never had much in common. He was a sentimentalist. He hung himself for selling out Jesus.

PROSECUTOR (*moving and perching himself on his table down* L.). Tell us, Mr Sadoc, when did you start your investigation?

SADOC. I went on the case the day after the body disappeared. By then the garden was quiet. The crowd was gone.

PROSECUTOR. Did you find any of his disciples around the tomb?

SADOC. No, sir. They were on their way to Galilee.

PROSECUTOR. Galilee?

SADOC. There were rumours that the Master had risen and would meet them in Galilee. I found only the usual curiosity-seekers. I asked them questions. I got vague answers about some strangers dressed in white.

PROSECUTOR. Dressed in white?

SADOC. Yes, sir. (*He clicks his fingers.*) But I discarded the strangers. Why would grave robbers make themselves conspicuous in white robes? The weirdest stories were in circulation—that an earthquake had rolled away the stone. (*He clicks his fingers.*) I discarded the earthquake. Why should it pick out this particular stone to move? Then there was a lot of talk about heavenly messengers. Angels with shining faces. (*He clicks his fingers.*) I discarded the angels.

PROSECUTOR (*a little impatiently*). Was there anything you did not discard, Mr Sadoc?

SADOC. The gardener. He was living there, a few steps from the spot. I established without any doubt that he was digging something the night before. So I kept an eye on him and went on asking questions.

PROSECUTOR. Whom did you question?

SADOC. Myself!

PROSECUTOR. Eh?

SADOC. That's my favourite method—asking questions of myself, and answering them. It sometimes brings surprising results. I asked myself what I would do if I were the grave robber.

PROSECUTOR. And what did you answer yourself?

SADOC. The answer is simple. It was dawn. I couldn't get far with the body. I couldn't take the chance of being caught with a corpse. So I'd bury it somewhere nearby.

PROSECUTOR. So you searched the garden?

SADOC. I saved myself a lot of trouble by thinking first. I discovered something very odd. The water canal was freshly filled. Why—I asked myself? Irrigation wasn't necessary. The soil was still wet from rain. There had been a cloudburst right after the crucifixion.

PROSECUTOR (*eagerly*). Go ahead. What happened then?

SADOC. I went on asking questions of myself. If there was no need for irrigation, why did I flood the canal? I had it!

PROSECUTOR. What?

SADOC. I trapped myself! (*He pauses.*) The rest was simple. I drained the canal; started to dig, and found the body.

PROSECUTOR (*rising; after a pause*). What body?

SADOC. The body of Jesus of Nazareth.

(*There is sensation in the courtroom.*)

PROSECUTOR (*triumphantly*). Thank you, Mr Sadoc. (*He moves to his chair down* L. *and sits.*) Your witness, Counsellor.

(*The* COUNSELLOR *rises and moves* C. *Despite the development, he is strangely calm.*)

COUNSELLOR. Tell us, Mr Sadoc, who beside yourself was present when the body was discovered?

SADOC. Two policemen.

COUNSELLOR. No private spectators at all?

SADOC (*acidly*). We didn't issue invitations. A police investigation is not a show.

COUNSELLOR (*after a pause*). So there weren't any unofficial witnesses present?

SADOC. I have already said so.

COUNSELLOR. And you had to follow instructions?

SADOC (*annoyed*). Like in any other case, Mr Counsellor.

COUNSELLOR. And your instructions were to find a body?

SADOC (*irritably*). Not *a* body—*the* body.

COUNSELLOR. And did you identify it as the body of Jesus of Nazareth?

SADOC. Beyond all doubt.

COUNSELLOR. Did you receive a high fee for your services, Mr Sadoc?

SADOC. I have a set price.

COUNSELLOR. Was there a bonus involved if you produced the desired result?

PROSECUTOR (*rising*). Objection!

JUDGE. Sustained!

(*The* PROSECUTOR *sits.*)

COUNSELLOR (*after a pause*). I ask you again, did you have any doubt about the identity of the body?

SADOC. Not the slightest.

COUNSELLOR (*after a pause*). Did you ever see Jesus of Nazareth alive?

SADOC. Many times. The night he was arrested. The day he

C

was sentenced to death. And finally, I saw him nailed to the cross.

COUNSELLOR. Then you were present at the crucifixion?

SADOC. Yes, I was there.

COUNSELLOR (*moving down* C.). From the beginning to the end?

SADOC. Just for a while. It wasn't the sort of spectacle one likes to see to the finish. Besides, it became dark. Storm clouds were gathering. I didn't want to get wet.

COUNSELLOR. So you left early?

SADOC. About in the middle.

COUNSELLOR (*moving down* R.; *after a pause*). Describe the body you found.

SADOC (*matter-of-factly*). It was the body of a man in his thirties. About five feet eight inches. He had pale parchment-like skin, a dark beard. . . .

COUNSELLOR. How much did the body weigh?

SADOC. Well—I would guess it somewhat under a hundred and thirty pounds.

COUNSELLOR. A hundred and thirty? Surely more than that?

SADOC (*with a superior air*). You seem to forget, Mr Counsellor, that he was on the cross.

COUNSELLOR (*moving* C.). Thank you. (*He pauses.*) Were his wounds very serious?

SADOC. They were caused by big, strong nails—spikes at least half-inch in diameter. The wounds showed that clearly.

COUNSELLOR. Did you examine them?

SADOC. That's the first thing I did. I examined them very thoroughly.

COUNSELLOR. Each one?

SADOC. Yes. The two on his hands, and the two on his feet.

COUNSELLOR. You examined each one separately?

SADOC. Yes. All four of them.

COUNSELLOR (*after a pause; abruptly*). But Jesus had five wounds.

SADOC (*taken aback; after a pause*). Five?

COUNSELLOR. Yes, Mr Sadoc. Just before he was taken down from the cross, a soldier pierced his side. You shouldn't have left so early.

SADOC (*trying to regain his poise*). Well, sir, of course I was mainly concerned with the nail wounds. It's possible that I may have overlooked some . . .

COUNSELLOR. A very lame excuse, Mr Sadoc. The fifth wound gave you away. The body you produced was not that of Jesus of Nazareth.

PROSECUTOR (*rising*). Objection!

JUDGE. Sustained.

COUNSELLOR. No more questions. (*He moves to his chair down* R. *and sits.*)

PROSECUTOR (*moving* C.). But I have some. Mr Sadoc, in what condition did you find the body?

SADOC. It was unwrapped. As you know, the burial cloths were left behind in the tomb.

PROSECUTOR. Then the body was covered with earth?

SADOC. Entirely. Wet, clayey earth. It stuck to the skin. Especially to the chest between the hollows of the ribs.

PROSECUTOR (*moving down* C.; *his back to the audience*). I see. Well —if there was a wound between the ribs, would you have seen it?

SADOC. Not necessarily. As I said, I was only interested in the wounds on the hands and the feet.

PROSECUTOR. Why just those four?

SADOC. Because they are the main characteristics of a crucified body.

PROSECUTOR. Indeed they are. (*He moves* C.) And what did you do after discovering the body?

SADOC. I delivered it to the authorities.

PROSECUTOR. What did they do with it?

SADOC. They exhibited the body publicly. People passed by and identified it.

PROSECUTOR. Did they recognize Jesus of Nazareth?

SADOC. Of course they did. At least, very many of them. They had seen him when he entered Jerusalem riding a donkey.

PROSECUTOR. And among all those people, no-one denied it was Jesus?

SADOC. No. They looked at him and filed out silently.

PROSECUTOR. So you can testify that not a single person doubted his identity?

SADOC. Definitely.

PROSECUTOR. That is all. (*He moves to his chair down* L. *and sits.*) Your witness, Counsellor.

(*The* COUNSELLOR *rises and moves* C.)

COUNSELLOR. Tell us, Mr Sadoc, was the body viewed by a large crowd?

SADOC. There was a long line.

COUNSELLOR. The same crowd that shouted for his crucifixion?

SADOC. I didn't know them personally. They were the people of Jerusalem.

COUNSELLOR. Were there any followers of Jesus among them?

SADOC. About a hundred, I guess.

COUNSELLOR. How could you tell if you didn't know them personally?

SADOC. They are easily recognized. If a poor man looks happy, he is a Christian.

COUNSELLOR (*after a pause*). You mean, they looked happy in the presence of their Master's dead body?

SADOC. I didn't say that! Please don't twist my words around. What I mean is—they didn't cry loudly.

COUNSELLOR. Were they intimidated, perhaps?

SADOC. They knew very well that the thing was over. The best they could do was to keep quiet and go.

COUNSELLOR. They were free to go?

SADOC. Well. . . .

COUNSELLOR. They were free to go?

SADOC. Yes.

COUNSELLOR. But they were kept under surveillance.

SADOC. We covered their movements, of course. We had to take every precaution.

COUNSELLOR. All over the country?

SADOC. It wasn't necessary. Christians live like sheep—in flocks. Most of them went to Galilee.

COUNSELLOR (*sharply*). Why?

SADOC. I didn't ask.

COUNSELLOR. But you just testified they went to Galilee to meet their risen Master.

SADOC. That was just wishful thinking.

COUNSELLOR. Was it? (*He pauses.*) If they believed the body you showed them was really Jesus, why should they go to Galilee to keep an appointment with him?

SADOC. I'm not a mind reader.

COUNSELLOR. I will tell you. They knew that the dead man was *not* Jesus. He was alive. He had risen and was waiting for them.

PROSECUTOR (*rising*). Objection!

JUDGE. Sustained!

COUNSELLOR. No more questions.

PROSECUTOR. One moment, Mr Sadoc. The followers of Jesus were mostly Galileans?

SADOC. Yes, sir.

PROSECUTOR. So to get home they would have to go back to Galilee in any case—regardless of whether he was risen or not?

SADOC. Yes, sir.

PROSECUTOR (*to the* COUNSELLOR). That's all I wanted. Your witness.

COUNSELLOR (*after a pause*). No more questions. (*He moves to his table down* R.)

PROSECUTOR. That's all, Mr Sadoc, and thanks very much.

(SADOC *rises, moves to the door* L. *and exits.*)

(*To the* JUDGE.) Your Honour, the State rests. (*He sits.*)

(*A tense hush falls over the courtroom, then the* JUDGE *turns to the* COUNSELLOR.)

JUDGE. Is the Defence ready?

COUNSELLOR. Yes, Your Honour. (*He pauses.*) I move that the indictment as charged be dismissed on the ground that no proof has been offered.

PROSECUTOR (*rising*). The State objects, Your Honour, on the ground that guilt has been conclusively proved.

JUDGE (*after a pause*). Objection sustained. Motion denied.

(*The* PROSECUTOR *sits. The* COUNSELLOR *moves* C.)

COUNSELLOR. May it please the Court—ladies and gentlemen of the Jury. The State has delivered its charge. The attack was well-calculated, vicious, sponsored by splendid hatred. But it was a cross-eyed attack. The Prosecutor, while fixing his glance on the gardener, kept his eyes constantly on Jesus. Every question was aimed at him—every word carried the implication that he is the real defendant at this trial. (*He pauses.*) It is a very clever attempt to disguise the weakness of the Prosecution's case against the gardener. But by making Jesus his target, my opponent knows he can count on powerful assistance. The assistance of—doubt. The weapon against—faith. A brilliant advocate of reason, my opponent is well aware of its strength. (*He pauses and smiles pensively.*) But faith is here, ladies and gentlemen—here and presenting his case. A strange contradiction—faith giving evidence. Throwing the immeasurable on the scales of justice. But I believe that this scale is sensitive. I believe in the instrument of trial. And I believe in the Twelve—(*he breaks down* C.)—and this time I don't mean the disciples—I mean—(*he gives a slight bow to the audience*)—the Jury. To this Jury, the Defence will prove that the gardener, Yahuda Jacobson, did not steal the body of Jesus of Nazareth on the night of April eighth. (*He pauses.*) It was Jesus himself who broke the bondage of death. It was life that burst open the tomb and hurled away the stone. It was the Master who walked on that morning—walked through the awakening spring—on the first Sunday of Man.

(*A deep silence falls over the courtroom. A silence almost tangible. The* COUNSELLOR *moves quietly to* L. *of his table, turns, then calls his first witness.*)

Susanna of Canaan.

GUARD (*rising, opening the door* R. *and calling*). Susanna of Canaan.

(SUSANNA *enters* R. *She is a woman in her thirties. Simple, humble, there is a sadness in her eyes. Obviously out of her element, she is awed by court procedure and seems very frightened. A black kerchief covers her hair and a large black shawl her shoulders.*)

COUNSELLOR. Will you take the stand, please.

(SUSANNA *crosses to the witness stand, and after being sworn, sits. The* GUARD *closes the door and sits.*)

(*He moves* R.C.) Susanna—you were one of the women who followed Jesus from Galilee?

SUSANNA (*sighing*). Yes, sir. I followed him to the very end.

COUNSELLOR. Will you tell the Jury what happened early in the morning on that first day of the week?

SUSANNA. Some of us women had arranged to meet at dawn. It was still dark when I joined them.

COUNSELLOR. Who were they?

SUSANNA. Mary Cleophas, Joanna, Salome, Mary Magdalen and some others I don't know by name.

COUNSELLOR. Did you all start out together?

SUSANNA. That's right, sir. We headed for the tomb. We walked silently. We were afraid to talk.

COUNSELLOR. Afraid? Why?

SUSANNA. There was something we didn't dare to speak of. (*Hesitantly.*) Finally, Mary said it for us.

COUNSELLOR. Mary Magdalen?

SUSANNA. No—it was Mary Cleophas, an aunt of Jesus. She knew him since he was a baby. "What a promising boy he was," she said. (*Wistfully.*) If only he had stuck to his father's trade, he would have been a good carpenter. He wouldn't have died so young either, and in such disgrace—like a criminal, between two thieves.

COUNSELLOR. Oh—you think he'd have done better as a carpenter. Then did you bury your faith with him?

SUSANNA. All we had left was sorrow.

COUNSELLOR. You gave up hope?

SUSANNA. We all saw him die.

COUNSELLOR (*moving down L.*). Still—you went to the tomb. Why? Was it to help the gardener steal the body?

SUSANNA (*shocked*). No!

COUNSELLOR. But a witness heard Mary Magdalen talk to the women about moving the stone.

SUSANNA. Yes, it's true. All we wanted was to anoint the body with sweet spices—after the Sabbath was over.

COUNSELLOR (*moving to* SUSANNA; *emphatically*). Then the only purpose of the morning visit was a last ministry?

SUSANNA. Yes, sir.

COUNSELLOR (*after a pause*). Susanna, please tell the Jury what you saw in the garden.

SUSANNA (*after a pause*). When we got there, the sun was just coming up. We'd hardly stepped on the grounds when Mary Magdalen shouted—"Look—the tomb is open! The stone is rolled away!" She tore herself from us and ran back towards the city to tell Peter and John.

COUNSELLOR. Without waiting to find out what had happened?

SUSANNA. Magdalen was always like that. Quick, nervous, excited. So we didn't try to stop her and just went up to the tomb.

COUNSELLOR. Did you see the gardener there?

SUSANNA. No, sir. He wasn't around.

COUNSELLOR. Did you call out for him?

SUSANNA. We were just going to, when suddenly . . . (*She breaks off.*)

COUNSELLOR. Go on—go on. What was it that happened suddenly?

SUSANNA. We saw a man.

COUNSELLOR. Who was it?

SUSANNA. A young man dressed in a white robe—a robe as white as snow.

COUNSELLOR. What was he doing there?

SUSANNA. Sitting on the stone before the tomb. He seemed to be waiting for us.

COUNSELLOR. Did you ask him what he wanted?

SUSANNA. We didn't ask anything, sir. We were much too frightened.

COUNSELLOR. Why?

SUSANNA (*simply*). Because he was an angel.

COUNSELLOR (*smiling*). Is an angel so frightening?

SUSANNA (*re-living the experience; raptly*). His face was like lightning. We hardly dared look at him. We felt that something wonderful had happened, and bowed our faces to the ground.

COUNSELLOR. Didn't you tell him why you had come?

SUSANNA. We couldn't speak at first. Then somehow we got ourselves together and told him we came for the body of Jesus of Nazareth.

COUNSELLOR. And what did the angel say to that?

SUSANNA. He said, "Jesus is not here. He is risen."

COUNSELLOR (*tensely*). Susanna, it is very important that you remember everything exactly as it happened. Please repeat to the Jury word for word what the angel said.

SUSANNA (*firmly*). He said, "Jesus is not here. He is risen."

COUNSELLOR. "Risen"! That was the word. Are you sure?

SUSANNA. Yes, sir. That was the word.

COUNSELLOR. Thank you, Susanna. I have no more questions. (*He moves to his chair down* R. *and sits. To the* PROSECUTOR.) Your witness.

(*The* PROSECUTOR *rises. He approaches the witness stand with such aggressive belligerence that* SUSANNA, *already flustered, shrinks back in her seat.*)

PROSECUTOR. Susanna—it must be quite an experience to meet an angel.

SUSANNA. I'll never get over it, sir.

PROSECUTOR. Won't you tell us some more

SUSANNA. I've told everything.

PROSECUTOR. Well, now, Susanna, you've given a rather sketchy account for such an important event You don't meet an angel every day, or do you? (*Maliciously.*) Haven't you forgotten a detail or two?

SUSANNA (*uneasily*). Sir, all of us were trembling. We didn't look around. We just stared into the empty tomb.

PROSECUTOR (*moving down* L.). And what about the angel?

SUSANNA. He was sitting on the right hand side.

PROSECUTOR. On the right hand side of what?

SUSANNA. The place where the body had been.

PROSECUTOR. Inside the tomb?

SUSANNA. Yes, sir.

PROSECUTOR. But you just said that the angel was sitting *outside* on the stone.

SUSANNA. Yes, sir.

PROSECUTOR (*moving to* SUSANNA; *sharply*). Then why do you suddenly put him inside?

SUSANNA (*agitatedly*). Oh, excuse me, sir. You can understand. We were completely overcome.

PROSECUTOR. It seems you haven't quite recovered. I'm afraid you're confusing the Jury.

COUNSELLOR (*rising*). Your Honour, it is the Prosecutor who is confusing the Jury. The testimony of this woman is very clear.

JUDGE. Don't be so solicitous about the Jury, gentlemen. It is quite capable of making up its own mind. Proceed.

(*The* COUNSELLOR *sits.*)

PROSECUTOR (*breaking* C.; *bitingly*). Much as my esteemed opponent seems to resent it, I must insist on clarifying the position of this so-called angel. (*To* SUSANNA.) Please describe what you saw inside the tomb.

SUSANNA (*completely upset*). We just stood there—speechless with fear and joy. We couldn't take our eyes off the sheet. We could still see the imprint of his body. Then we heard the angels speaking to us. They said not to be afraid any more. The Master was on his way to Galilee.

PROSECUTOR (*after a pause*). The angels told you that?

SUSANNA. Yes, they did.

PROSECUTOR. They? What do you mean by *they*?

SUSANNA. The two angels.

PROSECUTOR (*moving down* C.). Our angel population seems to be increasing. Up to now we had only one. Now you are speaking about two. (*He moves to* SUSANNA. *Threateningly.*) You'd better make up your mind, Susanna. How many were they?

SUSANNA (*flustered*). Well, sir—I—I really . . .

PROSECUTOR. One or two?

SUSANNA. Two—yes, they were two.

PROSECUTOR. And what were your two angels doing?

SUSANNA. They stood there—with light all around them.

PROSECUTOR. Both stood there?

SUSANNA. Yes, sir.

PROSECUTOR (*quickly*). You just told us that one angel was sitting—on the right hand side. Now what do you expect me to believe?

SUSANNA (*after a pause; miserably*). They were both standing, sir.

PROSECUTOR (*with feigned exasperation*). All right. Then let's stick to that—before your angel, or is it angels, get us all mixed up. (*He pauses.*) Go ahead, please. How long did you stay in the tomb?

SUSANNA. We all left after a while—and hurried back to the city.

PROSECUTOR. Did the angels go with you?

SUSANNA. No, sir. They stayed behind.

PROSECUTOR. Inside the tomb?

SUSANNA. Yes, sir.

PROSECUTOR. Why? Were they guarding the place, perhaps.

SUSANNA. I don't know. Maybe they were. They just remained sitting there—one at the head and one at the foot where the body had lain.

PROSECUTOR (*exclaiming*). Sitting! I give up. A moment ago you testified they were standing! You should have rehearsed your story much better——

COUNSELLOR ⎱ (*together*). ⎰ (*Rising; vehemently.*) I object, Your Honour!

PROSECUTOR ⎰   ⎱ —you over-reached yourself.

COUNSELLOR. The State is insulting the witness. It is plain my opponent is afraid of the impact of this testimony. His only refuge is to discredit her.

JUDGE. Sustained! The State is cautioned to refrain from derogatory comment.

PROSECUTOR. Your Honour, the witness has discredited herself. She contradicts her testimony by giving us four different versions. (*In ridiculing tone.*) An angel outside—an angel inside—two angels standing—two angels sitting. The Defence might call this evidence. I call it fiction!

COUNSELLOR (*calmly*). With a very few questions I can turn this fiction into reality.

PROSECUTOR (*moving to his chair down L. and sitting*). Your witness.

(*The* COUNSELLOR *moves* C. *He smiles gently.*)

COUNSELLOR (*soothingly*). There is nothing to be frightened of, Susanna. Just compose yourself and answer my questions calmly.

SUSANNA (*her eyes moist with relief*). Thank you, sir. I will.

COUNSELLOR. You told us you saw an angel sitting on the stone outside the tomb.

SUSANNA. Yes, sir.

COUNSELLOR. And what did you see inside the tomb?

SUSANNA. Another angel was sitting there.

COUNSELLOR. A different angel?

SUSANNA. That's right, sir.

COUNSELLOR. Why didn't you tell that to the Prosecutor?

Susanna. I didn't have a chance. He asked his questions in a way that whatever I answered was wrong.

Counsellor (*after a pause*). Well, let's get it straight now. One angel was outside, and the other inside.

Susanna. That's how it was, sir.

Counsellor (*turning to the* Prosecutor). That accounts for the two angels, Mr Prosecutor. (*He turns to* Susanna.) Now, for the sake of clarity, give each angel a number. Angel number one outside. Angel number two inside. (*He looks at the* Prosecutor.) Even the State will understand that.

(*A low giggle ripples through the courtroom. Having scored his point, the* Counsellor *turns back to* Susanna.)

Now then, Susanna, we know that angel number one was inside the tomb.

Susanna. Yes, sir. He was sitting.

Counsellor. All the time you were there?

Susanna. No, sir. When angel number one entered the tomb, he stood up.

Counsellor (*turning to the* Prosecutor). Well, Mr Prosecutor, there you have your two angels standing. They weren't marble angels. They could change positions—come and go—sit and stand. (*He turns to* Susanna.) And what happened as you left the tomb?

Susanna (*relieved*). Both angels sat down.

Counsellor (*turning to the* Prosecutor). Please note, Mr Prosecutor—our two angels are now sitting. Is there anything confusing about it? Only for one who deliberately wishes to create confusion. (*He turns to the audience.*) Ladies and gentlemen of the Jury—Susanna's testimony is clear and unmistakable. What the State calls four different versions are one very simple story—the truth. (*He turns to* Susanna.) No more questions. (*He moves to his chair down* R. *and sits.*)

Prosecutor (*rising quickly; to* Susanna). Before you step down, please tell me—did you ever see angels before?

Susanna. Never.

Prosecutor. So that was the very first time?

Susanna. Yes, sir.

Prosecutor (*moving* R. *of his table*). Then how did you know they were angels?

Susanna. I knew it.

Prosecutor. How? Did they wear signs marked—angel?

Susanna. They wore white robes.

Prosecutor. A white robe doesn't make an angel.

Susanna. There was light on their faces.

Prosecutor. You saw them at sunrise, didn't you?

Susanna. Yes, sir.

Prosecutor. Then that light on their faces could have come from the sun.

SUSANNA. It was a different sort of light.

PROSECUTOR. Did they have wings?

SUSANNA. I didn't notice any.

PROSECUTOR. So actually, you are the one who made angels out of them.

SUSANNA. No, sir. No-one can tell me any different. (*To the audience.*) They *were* angels.

PROSECUTOR. Perhaps they introduced themselves. Gave you their name and rank. I am Gabriel, arch-angel of the Lord—or Michael, or Raphael, or whatever . . .

SUSANNA. No, sir. They didn't tell us their names.

PROSECUTOR (*moving* C.). Well, Susanna—if I could believe any part of what you have told us here, I'd agree that you did see a couple of strangers dressed in white. Most likely the gardener's accomplices who helped him snatch the body. (*Arbitrarily.*) But they were not angels!

COUNSELLOR (*rising*). Objection!

JUDGE. Sustained!

PROSECUTOR (*moving to his chair down* L. *and sitting*). No more questions.

(SUSANNA *rises, moves to the door* L. *and exits. The* COUNSELLOR *calls the next witness.*)

COUNSELLOR. Professor Adronicus Thaddeus.

GUARD (*rising, opening the door* R. *and calling*). Professor Adronicus Thaddeus.

(THADDEUS *enters* R. *and crosses to the witness stand. He is an old man and wears a crushed suit and rumpled necktie. He has a shock of grey hair. He is nimble and alert, with quick eyes and a gratifying smile. He is a great scientist who has always remained a schoolboy.*)

COUNSELLOR. Will you take the stand please.

(*After being sworn,* THADDEUS *sits. The* GUARD *closes the door and sits.*)

(*He moves to* L. *of his table down* R. *and perches himself on the edge of it.*) Professor Thaddeus, you are an expert on angels?

THADDEUS. I am considered so, sir.

COUNSELLOR. Will you state your qualifications.

THADDEUS. I studied angelology—the science of angels. It is collateral to my main subject.

COUNSELLOR. And what is that subject?

THADDEUS. I am a professor of cosmogony.

COUNSELLOR. Will you kindly explain that?

THADDEUS. It is a sort of pantheognostical evolutionism—or, astrologically speaking, the geneology of the galactic stellar system.

PROSECUTOR (*interjecting*). I'm afraid we need an interpreter.

JUDGE. Can the witness express himself more simply?

THADDEUS (*rising*). Yes, Your Honour. All those sciences deal with one question. What makes the world run?

COUNSELLOR. Have you found the answer?

THADDEUS. According to the most recent discoveries of science, the world is run by God. (*He resumes his seat.*)

COUNSELLOR. I am glad you found that out.

THADDEUS. It took us quite a while. We scientists spent our lives searching for truth we had as children, and that was the only answer. There must be an author—an author of life.

COUNSELLOR (*rising and moving* c.). And this truth led you to the science of angels?

THADDEUS. It gave a new aspect to my search for the Beginning. With God as the final conclusion, all mythical elements of Genesis are restored to authority. There is a divine organization in which angels are constantly employed.

COUNSELLOR. Thank you, Professor. The preceding witness testified that she met an angel dressed in a white robe, and since reference to angels is rather unusual at a trial, I'd like you to give the Jury your opinion. (*He breaks down* R.C.) Can we consider angels as a reality?

THADDEUS. Of course. If there is any reluctance in admitting this, it is merely prejudice against the name. The word angel reminds most people of murals, oil prints, stained-glass windows. But from a strictly scientific point of view, there is no reason whatever to assume that man is the highest degree of creature. There are creatures above our conception of space and time: angels. We shouldn't be afraid of the naïveté of the name. I can call them astro-intellects, or meta-organisms. It might sound more impressive, but I am afraid that the Prosecutor again will ask for an interpreter.

COUNSELLOR. Then let's agree to call them angels, Professor. And now, it is your opinion that those men at the tomb—those men in white—were angels?

THADDEUS (*deliberating*). The place of their appearance strongly inclines me to believe that they were—on guard duty on the boundary of life and death. Angels have many functions according to the offices they hold. Most of them, however, are carriers of executive orders.

COUNSELLOR. Tell us, Professor, since the State brought it up—when angels appear, do they have to wear wings?

THADDEUS. Not as a rule. (*He warms to his subject.*) And at this point I would like (*he rises and moves down* L.C.)—to rectify a widespread misunderstanding. Angels do not need their wings to fly. Calculations of aerodynamics prove that angel wings serve no mechanical purpose. They are symbols of a higher sphere. But when angels contact mortals, in most cases they come down in plain clothes.

COUNSELLOR (*moving to* THADDEUS *and leading him back to the witness stand*). Then applying your broad knowledge to the subject in hand, will you testify that angels do not have to appear in wings?

THADDEUS. Definitely. (*He resumes his seat on the witness stand.*)

COUNSELLOR (*easing* C.). And will you testify that those men in white robes were angels?

THADDEUS (*after a pause; cautiously*). I can state this much with absolute safety: the absence of wings does not bar them from being angels.

COUNSELLOR. Thank you, Professor. No more questions. (*He moves to his chair down* R. *and sits. To the* PROSECUTOR.) Your witness.

(*The* PROSECUTOR *rises and moves* C.)

PROSECUTOR (*after a pause*). Angelology must be a fascinating science. But there is one thing wrong with it. Tell us, Professor, do angels really exist?

THADDEUS (*offended*). Do you think, sir, I would spend a lifetime studying non-existing creatures?

PROSECUTOR (*after a pause*). Many lives have been spent in fancy.

THADDEUS (*categorically*). You cannot fancy something which has never been. The human mind cannot draw pictures out of nothing. The model for imagination is experience—individual or ancestral. The very fact that we can envision angels is proof of their existence.

PROSECUTOR. Your theories are intriguing—but not very convincing evidence. (*Sarcastically.*) If angels existed, wouldn't the Defence put one on the stand?

THADDEUS (*seriously*). It is not for us to summon angels—it is for them to summon us.

PROSECUTION (*derisively*). With the trumpet?

THADDEUS (*with an enigmatic smile*). One never knows the instrument, sir.

PROSECUTOR. That will do, Professor. (*He moves to his chair down* L. *and sits.*) No more questions.

(THADDEUS *rises, moves briskly to the door* L. *and exits. The* COUNSELLOR *rises and calls the next witness.*)

COUNSELLOR. Miss Mary Magdalen.

GUARD (*rising, opening the door* R. *and calling*). Miss Mary Magdalen.

(MARY MAGDALEN *enters* R. *and crosses to the witness stand. She is a woman in her late twenties, and is not the sinful beauty that tradition describes. More than beautiful, she is compelling—a woman who carries destiny with more charm than dream. Although of heroic temperament, her ecstasy becomes evident only in a few high moments of the testimony.*)

Most of the time she is well controlled and calm. Her smile has a touch of melancholy, her voice a timbre of the sensual. Her skin is white, and she has red hair, of course. It would be an irreverence against our heritage to give her hair any other colour. She is simply dressed, emphasizing the fact that she is above all feminine vanity, exposing with this very emphasis that there is still vanity in her. Her simple dress is carefully chosen. It has fashion and line.)

COUNSELLOR. Will you take the stand please.

(After MAGDALEN *has been sworn, she sits. The* GUARD *closes the door and sits.)*

(He moves C.*)* Miss Magdalen—I am going to ask you a question, and I wish you to weigh your reply very carefully. Did you or did you not see angels in the tomb of Jesus?

MAGDALEN *(after a pause).* I did.

COUNSELLOR. How many?

MAGDALEN. Two.

COUNSELLOR. The State is attempting to create a great doubt in this regard. Are you positive it was angels you saw?

MAGDALEN. There was a radiance around them I couldn't possibly misunderstand.

COUNSELLOR. Thank you. Now will you tell the Jury exactly what happened that first Sunday morning in the garden.

MAGDALEN *(after a pause).* By the time I came back, the other women were gone. You know I left them as soon as we arrived—at daybreak.

COUNSELLOR. That has already been testified. You ran with the news to Peter and John, and you all returned—together.

MAGDALEN. Peter and John hurried ahead—I followed at a distance. They went straight into the tomb. I waited outside.

COUNSELLOR. And what did you do?

MAGDALEN. I was crying, I think. Then after a while I saw Peter and John come out of the tomb. They seemed to be in a daze. I asked them what had happened, but they didn't hear me.

COUNSELLOR. They passed you by without answering?

MAGDALEN. Not a word. They left the garden as if walking in a dream. *(She pauses.)* I was alone.

COUNSELLOR. And then, did you enter the tomb?

MAGDALEN. I looked into it. *(She pauses.)*

COUNSELLOR *(gently).* Go on, please.

MAGDALEN. A shadow fell before me on the grass—the shadow of a man. He stood behind me. I felt his glance on my shoulders. Then he asked in a low voice why I was crying.

COUNSELLOR. Who was this man?

MAGDALEN. First, I thought it was the gardener. I turned to him and told him—"Sir, if you took the body of my Lord away, would you kindly tell me where it is laid!" He looked at me and smiled. "Mary," he said. "Master," I cried out, and fell on my knees. Because he was Jesus.

COUNSELLOR. The same Jesus who died three days before?

MAGDALEN. The same!

COUNSELLOR. Not a shadow?

MAGDALEN. No!

COUNSELLOR. Not a vision—not a ghost?

MAGDALEN. Ghosts don't walk in daylight—it was broad daylight—a glorious spring morning. The garden was flooded with sunshine.

COUNSELLOR (*carried away*). Then you saw him clearly? Him—Jesus alive!

PROSECUTOR (*rising*). Objection! Is Counsel giving evidence now?

COUNSELLOR (*turning to the* PROSECUTOR). I am merely stating facts given by the witness.

PROSECUTOR (*sarcastically*). We will prove that the witness is a woman with a vivid imagination—unable to distinguish between facts and fantasies.

JUDGE (*rapping with his gavel*). Objection overruled. Proceed.

(*The* PROSECUTOR *sits.*)

COUNSELLOR. Mary Magdalen—you were the first to see the risen Jesus?

MAGDALEN (*after a pause; with humble pride*). He was good and gracious to grant me this distinction. It was the Master's gentle answer.

COUNSELLOR. Answer to what?

MAGDALEN. My love.

COUNSELLOR. Your love must be great.

MAGDALEN. Before anyone else, he showed himself to me. He was so close I could have touched him.

COUNSELLOR. And did you?

MAGDALEN. He asked me not to. But as I reached out my arms I could feel the warmth of life. He had the warmth of a child just born.

(*There is a pause.*)

COUNSELLOR. Have you ever had a child, Magdalen?

MAGDALEN. No—I've never been married.

COUNSELLOR. Where were you born?

MAGDALEN. Magdala, in Galilee. That's how I got my name.

COUNSELLOR. And how long did you live there?

MAGDALEN. The first sixteen years of my life.

COUNSELLOR. Will you tell us something about those early years?

PROSECUTOR (*rising*). Objection, Your Honour. The life story of the witness is irrelevant and immaterial.

Counsellor. Your Honour! Mary Magdalen is the great witness to the resurrection. The very foundation of our belief. The life of this woman must stand clearly before the Jury. If I don't ask these questions, the Prosecutor will. He is waiting eagerly his turn. (*With sarcasm.*) The Defence is convinced that Magdalen will pass the test. She will prove herself to be what she is—the first lady of that Easter morning.

Judge. The Court already has ruled that questions concerning character are permitted. Proceed.

(*The* Prosecutor *sits.*)

Counsellor (*easing down* r.c.). Well, Magdalen—will you tell us about your childhood?

Magdalen (*after a pause*). I am afraid there isn't much to tell. I grew up like the other girls in Magdala—a small town among the hills of Galilee. Pastures, orchards, white houses, a synagogue, and a general store.

Counsellor. What was your father?

Magdalen. An elder of the synagogue, and owner of the general store. His life was divided between God and the business.

Counsellor. And your mother?

Magdalen (*after a pause*). She was pregnant—all her life. If it was a boy, father slaughtered a lamb and gave a banquet with wine.

Counsellor. With girls he gave no banquets?

Magdalen. And no wine. The men of Israel wanted sons. Every day they praised the Lord for not making them women.

Counsellor. That was written in the prayers?

Magdalen. Clearly written. They looked upon us as second-rate creatures. In the synagogue we had to sit separately. God belonged to the men. They served God in the kitchen by preparing food according to law.

Counsellor. You must have grown up with a sense of inferiority.

Magdalen. The excuse for our being was to give them sons. (*She pauses.*) When I was sixteen, mother died trying to give father another son. (*She pauses.*) I knew then I would never live the life she had lived. I had to be free. There was a white road winding into the distance. Travelling salesmen came bringing merchandise. Silks, spices, perfumes—I loved the perfumes—they had the scent of far-away cities.

Counsellor. And tell us, how did you leave your father's house?

Magdalen. One day father told me to bake a mince pie because Zachary, the blacksmith, was coming to dinner. After dinner, father left us alone. I became frightened. Zachary said that he wanted to marry me. He said that I had everything he wanted in a woman. I was healthy, I had white skin, and I could bake a mince pie.

COUNSELLOR. What was your answer to his proposal?

MAGDALEN. Father had already decided for me. I just looked at Zachary—he was a big man—he had the heavy hand of a blacksmith. No matter how much he washed, there was charcoal under his nails. His eyes gleamed darkly when he looked at me. He wanted a son.

COUNSELLOR. And you, Magdalen?

MAGDALEN. I was thinking of mother. No—I said to myself. (*She pauses.*) Next morning I ran away.

COUNSELLOR. Where were you bound for?

MAGDALEN. I didn't know. I just ran for freedom. I didn't stop until I reached the fork in the road. There were two ways. One led into the wilderness—the other to Jerusalem.

COUNSELLOR. And which one did you choose?

MAGDALEN. I was afraid of the wilderness. I'd been told a wild man was living there, eating locusts, and crying in a terrifying voice. (*She pauses.*) So I went to Jerusalem. I had heard it was crowded with interesting strangers—men from distant countries.

COUNSELLOR. And did you meet them?

MAGDALEN (*after a pause; reluctantly*). Yes—I did.

COUNSELLOR. Were they pleased with you?

MAGDALEN. They thought I was intelligent—with a great sense for language. In a short time I spoke Latin and Greek. They liked my accent.

COUNSELLOR. During all this time, Magdalen, you never though you were doing wrong?

MAGDALEN. I wasn't thinking. I was free—that was all that counted.

COUNSELLOR. Then your life was just a protest against the oppressions of your childhood. Against the tyranny of your father. Against what we might rightly call—the servitude of women.

PROSECUTOR (*rising*). Objection, Your Honour. The Defence is trying to justify the looseness of this woman.

JUDGE. Objection overruled. Proceed.

(*The* PROSECUTOR *sits.*)

COUNSELLOR. Well, Miss Magdalen, will you tell us more about your new life.

MAGDALEN (*after a pause*). It was new, indeed. A new world.

COUNSELLOR. Did you travel?

MAGDALEN. Much. I was curious. Once a Roman diplomat took me to Alexandria. I saw Egypt. Not the Egypt of plagues. The Egypt of wonders. Rich, luxurious, sophisticated. I met poets, sculptors, philosophers. I only found out then how much I had to learn. I learned how to wear clothes, read books, and paint my toe-nails.

COUNSELLOR. Cosmetics?

D

MAGDALEN. And perfumes. I had all the perfume I ever wanted.
Egypt was a land of love. Cleopatra was dead, but her romance
lived on. And the fallen Anthony was still a God—the Great
Lover—the one in a lifetime, if a woman ever finds him.
COUNSELLOR. And did you find him in Egypt?
MAGDALEN. No. It was entirely my fault. To find a Great
Lover, you must have a great love to give. I didn't have it yet
(*She pauses.*) When I returned to Jerusalem, I was very tired.
COUNSELLOR. Why?
MAGDALEN (*after a pause*). When sin becomes a routine, it loses
its charm. The art of love-making turns dull without the final
fulfilment. For the first time I wanted a son. (*She breaks off.*)
COUNSELLOR. Please continue.
MAGDALEN (*after a pause*). But I was barren. (*She pauses.*) Barren
as the life I had lived. I just drifted on the surface. I had influen-
tial friends, excellent connections. I was invited to the Governor's pal ce, introduced at the royal court. King Herod liked gay
parties.
COUNSELLOR. Did you attend many of them?
MAGDALEN. Many. The King enjoyed entertainment. Greek
lute players, Persian magicians, dancers from India. There was
wrestling and fighting. Gladiators died under the sword. Herod
always found new amusements. One night he cut off the head of a
prophet.
COUNSELLOR. The man who cried in the wilderness?
MAGDALEN. I saw him. His head was on a golden plate—his
open eyes stared at me. (*She pauses. With a shiver.*) I had a complete breakdown. I couldn't stop laughing and crying.
COUNSELLOR. Was it very bad?
MAGDALEN. My friends gave me up—they thought I had gone
insane. Some quack examined me and said I was possessed by
seven devils. But between the spells I knew clearly what I wanted.
(*Wistfully.*) I wanted to go back to Galilee—to the hills from
which I had ran away—to the lonely mountainside.
COUNSELLOR. And did you go back, Magdalen?
MAGDALEN. I did. But the mountainside wasn't lonely any
more. A big crowd was gathered on the slope and a man was
talking to them. (*With suppressed excitement.*) His voice was low,
but carried far. I stood among the others and listened. The birds
fell silent when he talked. Not a leaf trembled. And when it was
over, I knew I had found the Great Lover.
COUNSELLOR. How could you tell? Could you get close to him?
MAGDALEN. I tried to—but the crowd was too big. I followed
him from town to town. And one evening when he was at dinner
at a rich man's house, the moment came. I took a box of perfumes—my most precious ones—and entered the dining-room.
COUNSELLOR. Uninvited?
MAGDALEN. No-one asked me—but I knew the Master expected

me. He was at the table, reclining on a couch—and wasn't surprised when he saw me. I kneeled and poured all my perfume over his feet. I didn't have to say a word. He understood me, I understood him. All that had happened in my life had been for one purpose—to understand him. (*Softly.*) Then his voice came—I was forgiven.

COUNSELLOR. And healed?

MAGDALEN. I was freed from my seven devils. I never left the Master. I walked with him through the country—on the edge of wheat fields—on the shores of the sea. When the end came, I walked with him to the cross. And on the morning he rose, I walked with him in the garden. He called me Mary as he had done so often before. He told me to meet him in Galilee.

COUNSELLOR. He told you that!

MAGDALEN. He went ahead. (*She rises.*) I looked after him. For one more moment I saw him as he walked among the trees—and then there was only sunshine.

COUNSELLOR. What did you do then?

MAGDALEN (*enraptured*). At first I saw only little things—a grasshopper jumped—a wasp droned—a lizard ran among the rocks. Only then did I realize. I ran towards the city. I went from house to house. Everyone! Listen to me! Jesus is risen! Yes—Risen! You must believe me—I saw him with my own eyes. Youthful and strong, standing over his grave. Don't be afraid. I bring good news. There is no death any more! Death died early this Sunday morning. From now on there is only life! Life—everlasting. (*Her voice breaks. She is overcome with tears.*)

(*The lights start to dim out. Over her joyful weeping the gentle voice of the* JUDGE *is heard.*)

JUDGE (*rapping with his gavel*). The Court orders a recess.

The LIGHTS *Black-Out as*—

the CURTAIN *falls.*

ACT III

SCENE.—*The same. The same night, just before dawn.*

When the CURTAIN *rises, the stage is in darkness. After a moment, the rapping of the gavel is heard and the lights come up. The* JUDGE, PROSECUTOR, COUNSELLOR, CLERK *and* GARDENER *are seated in their places. The trial continues.*

JUDGE (*to the* COUNSELLOR). Are you ready to continue with Miss Magdalen?

COUNSELLOR (*rising and moving* R.C.). In just a little while, Your Honour, if the Court will grant her a few more minutes to recover.

JUDGE. The Court cannot allow further delay. Proceed with your next witness until she is able to take the stand.

COUNSELLOR. Yes, Your Honour. (*He turns to the* GARDENER.) Mr Yahuda Jacobson, will you step forward.

(*The* GARDENER, *awkward and bewildered, rises and moves to the* COUNSELLOR.)

Will you take the stand.

(*The* GARDENER *moves to the witness stand and, after being sworn, sits.*)

Tell us, Mr Jacobson, when did you get up on the morning of April eighth?

GARDENER. I got up very early, sir.

COUNSELLOR. How early?

GARDENER. It was still dark.

COUNSELLOR. Did you go to work right away?

GARDENER (*somewhat amazed*). Oh, no, sir. I said my morning prayers first.

COUNSELLOR (*apologetically*). Of course—you are a devout Jew.

GARDENER (*simply*). I keep the commandments.

COUNSELLOR. And never miss your morning prayers?

GARDENER. Never.

COUNSELLOR. Would you mind if I asked you to recite them for us?

PROSECUTOR (*rising*). Objection! The prayers of the defendant are irrelevant.

COUNSELLOR (*to the* JUDGE). Your Honour, this God-fearing man is accused of a ghoulish crime. I call upon the words of his prayer to testify for him.

JUDGE. Objection overruled. Proceed.

(*The* PROSECUTOR *sits.*)

COUNSELLOR (*softly*). Go ahead, Mr Jacobson.

GARDENER. Sir, it's a long prayer to recite.

COUNSELLOR. Then give us just a part of it.

GARDENER. The Psalm. (*Reverently.*) "Let the Heavens rejoice, the earth be glad, and the trees exult before the Lord."

COUNSELLOR (*with gentle emphasis*). And with these words in your heart, you went out and snatched a body.

GARDENER. No, sir.

COUNSELLOR. Look at the Jury, Mr Jacobson, and tell them. Did you steal the body of Jesus of Nazareth?

GARDENER. I did not.

COUNSELLOR. Thank you. (*To the* PROSECUTOR.) Your witness. (*He moves to his chair down* R. *and sits.*)

(*The* PROSECUTOR *rises and eases down* L.)

PROSECUTOR. Mr Jacobson, a soldier testified here that you brought him wine during the night he was guarding the tomb—and then he fell asleep.

GARDENER. Yes, sir. That's true.

PROSECUTOR. Did you put a drug in that wine?

GARDENER. No, sir.

PROSECUTOR. Why did you give the soldier wine?

GARDENER (*after a short pause*). The poor fellow was cold. It was a chilly night. I felt sorry for him.

PROSECUTOR (*sceptically*). You want us to believe it was just pity? You were sorry for a strange soldier?

GARDENER (*simply*). I live by the Law, sir. "You should love the strangers within your gates."

PROSECUTOR (*smiling sarcastically*). Your Godliness is very commendable, Mr Jacobson. But I'm afraid you will have to answer some profane questions. After your morning devotions you took a shovel and dug a grave—did you not?

GARDENER. Yes, sir, I did.

PROSECUTOR. Why?

GARDENER. I had orders to bury Jesus in a final resting place—as soon as the Sabbath was over.

PROSECUTOR. At what time did you finish digging the grave?

GARDENER. Just as it was getting light.

PROSECUTOR. And what did you do then?

GARDENER (*simply*). I watched the grass grow.

PROSECUTOR (*sarcastically*). Strenuous work indeed, Mr Jacobson, but it couldn't have occupied *all* your attention.

GARDENER. My job is to watch the grass grow, sir. It was young grass, freshly sown.

PROSECUTOR. Let's keep horticulture out of this. When did you put the body into the grave?

GARDENER. I never put the body into the grave.

PROSECUTOR (*moving to the* GARDENER; *sharply*). You didn't! Then why did you fill it up? And in such a hurry.

GARDENER. There was no-one to bury. The body disappeared from the tomb.

PROSECUTOR. Did you look in the empty tomb?

GARDENER. Yes, sir.

PROSECUTOR. And did you see the angels?

GARDENER. No, sir.

PROSECUTOR (*smiling*). They were peculiar angels—(*he moves* R.C.)—they showed themselves only to females. Well, so you filled up the grave because there was no-one to put in it?

GARDENER. Yes, sir. I couldn't leave a hole in the garden.

PROSECUTOR. You are very fussy, Mr Jacobson. But I'm afraid you've overlooked something. You had an order to dig a grave?

GARDENER. Yes, sir.

PROSECUTOR (*abruptly*). Is it usual to dig a grave in the bed of a canal—and flood it with water?

GARDENER. No, sir.

PROSECUTOR. Then how did you happen to dig in that particular spot? Was that an order, too?

GARDENER. No, sir. I picked the spot myself.

PROSECUTOR. Why *that* particular spot?

GARDENER. I told you. I had a freshly planted lawn. I knew if word got around that Jesus was buried in our garden, folks would come to visit his grave—city folks. They would trample all over my lawn. Do you know how much work goes into a lawn? Ploughing against the rocky hillside—it takes a lot out of you before anything shows. (*Practically.*) So I figured if I laid him in a secret grave, people wouldn't come. He would have peace and quiet—and my grass would grow.

PROSECUTOR. Very touching—the simple, God-fearing gardener.

(*The* GUARD, *escorting* MARY MAGDALEN, *enters* R. *She is pale but composed.*)

You are a very smart man, Mr Jacobson. I have no more questions. (*He moves to his chair down* L. *and sits.*)

(*The* GUARD *moves to the* COUNSELLOR *and whispers to him. The* GARDENER *rises, moves to his chair at the table down* R. *and sits. The* COUNSELLOR *rises.*)

COUNSELLOR (*to the* JUDGE). Your Honour, Mary Magdalen is ready for cross-examination.

JUDGE. Proceed.

(*The* GUARD *moves to his chair up* R. *and sits.*)

COUNSELLOR (*to the* PROSECUTOR). Your witness. (*He sits.*)

PROSECUTOR (*rising; to* MAGDALEN). Will you take the stand, please.

(MAGDALEN *moves to the witness stand and sits.*)

(*He moves to* R. *of his table.*) Do you feel strong enough now to answer my questions?

MAGDALEN (*after a pause; resignedly*). I am ready.

PROSECUTOR. Your life story, Miss Magdalen, was very impressive. I followed it with extreme interest. As a matter of fact, I would like to hear more. Some of the details were mentioned very casually. For instance, what is your profession?

MAGDALEN (*after a pause*). I haven't any definite profession.

PROSECUTOR. Then what *indefinite* profession do you have?

MAGDALEN. I never learned any trade.

PROSECUTOR. Somewhat evasive, Miss Magdalen. You force me to speak bluntly. Are you a prostitute?

MAGDALEN (*gasping in horror*). Oh!

COUNSELLOR (*rising*). Don't be upset, Magdalen—you have nothing to hide.

MAGDALEN (*fiercely*). I am not!

(*The* COUNSELLOR *sits.*)

PROSECUTOR. You never slept with men for money?

MAGDALEN. Never!

PROSECUTOR (*unperturbed*). But you accepted gifts, didn't you?

MAGDALEN. Yes! I did.

PROSECUTOR. What kind of gifts? Were they trifles, or something a little more substantial? Like furs—jewels—or perhaps a villa and servants?

MAGDALEN (*scornfully*). You don't leave anything to imagination do you?

PROSECUTOR (*moving* C.). I leave imagination to the Defence; its case is based upon it. But you are too important a witness. We can't afford to give you the benefit of imagination. The life of a creed hangs upon your testimony. The Jury should know what kind of woman you are.

MAGDALEN. I've made mistakes—we all do.

PROSECUTOR. Don't escape in generalities. I want to know how you made your living.

MAGDALEN. I didn't walk the streets. Does that satisfy you?

PROSECUTOR. No? How did you meet your customers?

MAGDALEN (*angrily*). Why do you ask me all this? It has nothing to do with my testimony. My life is split in two parts. I don't want to remember the first.

PROSECUTOR. Well, whether you like it or not, you have to remember.

MAGDALEN (*violently*). No! That woman is dead! Even alive she was dead! (*She lowers her voice.*) It all happened before I met him.

PROSECUTOR. You mean before you developed a Jesus complex?

COUNSELLOR (*rising*). I object! The term, "Jesus complex", is derogatory to our faith.

PROSECUTOR (*to the* COUNSELLOR). Isn't your term rather a great name for an instinct? What is faith? A subconscious protest against death—a sedative for the rebellious human breast.

JUDGE (*rapping with his gavel*). Opposed counsel will kindly refrain from arguing over definitions. Objection overruled. Proceed.

(*The* COUNSELLOR *sits.*)

PROSECUTOR (*moving down* C.; *to the audience*). I think I have made my point, ladies and gentlemen. (*He breaks to* R. *of* MAGDALEN.) Let's turn the page to another chapter, Miss Magdalen. As a little girl, did you play with dolls?

MAGDALEN (*surprised*). I don't see any sense in that question.

PROSECUTOR. Please don't judge my questions—answer them. Did you play with dolls?

MAGDALEN. I didn't have much chance. As I told you, every year mother had another child.

PROSECUTOR. And you helped to take care of them?

MAGDALEN. Mother couldn't manage them alone. I put them to bed and told them stories until they fell asleep.

PROSECUTOR. Did you know many stories?

MAGDALEN. I made up new ones all the time.

PROSECUTOR. It was good training for your imagination. You had a lively imagination even then. Tell us, Miss Magdalen, how many children were there?

MAGDALEN. Twelve.

PROSECUTOR. I suppose you were the oldest.

MAGDALEN. Yes, I was.

PROSECUTOR. Did you often see your mother in labour?

MAGDALEN. The midwife was a frequent visitor. I warmed the water for her.

PROSECUTOR. How old was she?

COUNSELLOR (*rising*). Objection! The age of the midwife is irrelevant.

PROSECUTOR. The purpose of my question will be evident in a minute.

JUDGE. Objection overruled. Proceed.

(*The* COUNSELLOR *sits.*)

PROSECUTOR. Well, Miss Magdalen, was this midwife young and pretty?

MAGDALEN. She was an ugly old woman.

PROSECUTOR. An old witch?

MAGDALEN. You might call her that.

PROSECUTOR (*moving down* L.). So in your early youth you associated childbirth with the ugliness of an old woman—with agony and death.

MAGDALEN. Death?

PROSECUTOR. Didn't you see your mother dying in labour?

MAGDALEN. Yes, I did.

PROSECUTOR. And that gave you a phobia against child-bearing, didn't it?

MAGDALEN. I don't know.

PROSECUTOR. It must have. You ran away from home at sixteen. You refused marriage, you refused motherhood, (*he moves* c.) the dignity and destiny of women.

MAGDALEN. That's not true. In later years I wanted to have a child.

PROSECUTOR. I know—you so testified. But you couldn't have one.

MAGDALEN. I could not.

PROSECUTOR. Why not?

COUNSELLOR (*rising*). I object, Your Honour. The Defence has given the State great latitude. I listened to this line of questioning with the utmost indulgence. But now the Prosecutor is embarking on a physical check-up. . . .

PROSECUTOR. Your Honour, the testimony of this witness is of such import, that she must be mentally and physically flawless to give credence to her statements. No cross-examination can be thorough enough.

COUNSELLOR. This isn't cross-examination. The . . .

JUDGE (*rapping with his gavel*). Order, gentlemen. The State will refrain from questions intruding upon physical privacy. Objection sustained.

(*The* COUNSELLOR *sits.*)

PROSECUTOR (*after a pause*). Magdalen, were you ever confined to an insane asylum?

MAGDALEN. Never.

PROSECUTOR. Or treated privately for mental ailments?

MAGDALEN. No, I was not.

PROSECUTOR. But you did testify—and I am quoting you—that you were possessed by seven devils. Could that possibly mean anything else but insanity?

COUNSELLOR (*rising*). Objection!

PROSECUTOR. Your Honour, I speak merely as an interpreter. "Seven devils" are the witness's own words. I only translated them into colloquial.

JUDGE. Overruled. Proceed.

(*The* COUNSELLOR *sits.*)

PROSECUTOR. Well, Miss Magdalen, what would *you* call the mental state you were in?

MAGDALEN. I don't know how to name it. I simply realized that nothing could make sense. I was frustrated and empty. I couldn't go on. I had a complete breakdown.

PROSECUTOR. Brought on by a sense of guilt, I suppose.

MAGDALEN. A feeling of catastrophe—so deep, so violent—it almost choked me.

PROSECUTOR. Like a lump in your throat, was it?

MAGDALEN. Yes, I think it was.

PROSECUTOR. That certain hysterical lump in your throat. You couldn't swallow.

COUNSELLOR (rising). Objection! The Prosecutor has now turned into a psychiatrist.

JUDGE. Objection sustained.

(The COUNSELLOR sits.)

PROSECUTOR. Well, Miss Magdalen, you testified that you had recurrent crying spells. What was your condition after such attacks?

MAGDALEN. I just lay hours and hours in my bed in complete apathy, staring motionless at the ceiling.

PROSECUTOR. And what did you see on the ceiling?

MAGDALEN. Nothing. I mean, nothing but the usual things— little cracks, blisters, traces of moisture, peeling paint.

PROSECUTOR. Did they suggest anything to you? Did you make up patterns—figures—pictures?

MAGDALEN. Nothing definite. If you stare at a ceiling long enough, you begin to see all kinds of things—whatever you want to see.

PROSECUTOR. So you are blessed with the capacity to see whatever you want—a risen Jesus, for instance.

MAGDALEN. That's not true. At the time of my breakdown I didn't know there was a Jesus.

PROSECUTOR. But you were ready to meet one—ripe for the other extreme.

MAGDALEN. I was but a disciple at the Master's feet.

PROSECUTOR. Yes. You washed those feet with perfume—and dried them with your hair.

MAGDALEN. In supplication. It wasn't earthly love.

PROSECUTOR. What was it?

MAGDALEN (passionately). It was the dead craving for life. He gave me new life.

PROSECUTOR. And in return, you gave new life to him. It was you who raised him on that Easter morning! Your desire! Your fantasy!

MAGDALEN. That's a lie! A deliberate lie!

PROSECUTOR. You admitted it with your own words. The barren woman wanted to give birth. She couldn't deliver life, so she delivered a dream. Again you made up a story, Magdalen. A bedtime story for mankind. That they shouldn't be afraid of the dark.

MAGDALEN. It was no story. I saw him with my own eyes.

PROSECUTOR. Your eyes aren't capable of seeing reality, Magdalen. They can only project. They projected Jesus into the garden.

MAGDALEN (*firmly*). He was real—as real as the trees around him—as the hills beyond him—as the sun above him.

PROSECUTOR. Was he? I am quoting from your testimony again. You said you saw a man standing before you. *Not* Jesus—a man. First you thought it was the gardener.

MAGDALEN. Only for a moment.

PROSECUTOR. That moment was enough for you to transform him into Jesus. You were resolved to see Jesus, and you succeeded. Desire, love, hysteria, all teamed up to make the gardener the risen Christ.

MAGDALEN. He was the Master! However you twist it, no matter how much you want to, you can't send him back. No power on earth can seal that tomb again.

PROSECUTOR. That remains to be seen. Let's make a little test. Let's re-enact your meeting with the risen Master. (*He turns.*) May I ask the gardener to step forward?

(*The* GARDENER *rises, bewildered.*)

Step right here, Mr Jacobson.

(*The* GARDENER *moves to* R.C.)

Tell us, Miss Magdalen, how far from you was the man you believed to be Jesus?

MAGDALEN. Four or five steps.

PROSECUTOR (*measuring the distance from the witness stand to* C.). About here?

MAGDALEN. Yes.

PROSECUTOR. Will you please stand up, Miss Magdalen.

(MAGDALEN *rises.*)

Thank you. And would you turn your back to us please. I want to play this scene just as you described it. You were crying, weren't you? Then you suddenly realized that a man was standing behind you. His shadow fell upon the grass.

(*The lights dim down, all except a spotlight off* R., *shining on the* GARDENER, *so that he casts a shadow to* L. MAGDALEN *turns and faces* L. *The* PROSECUTOR *puts the* GARDENER *into position* C., *facing* L., *so that his shadow falls before* MAGDALEN *on the floor. The Court watches the procedure intently.*)

That ought to do it. Mr Jacobson, did you hear Miss Magdalen's testimony?

GARDENER. Yes, I did.

PROSECUTOR. Then you know your part. It's very simple. You ask her why she is crying. And when she turns to you and tells you, call her Mary—just as the supposed Jesus did. Is that clear?

GARDENER. Yes, sir.

PROSECUTOR. That's all. You start when I give the signal. (*He moves down* L.)

(*The Court waits in breathless silence.*)
Go ahead.

GARDENER (*after a pause; to* MAGDALEN). Woman, why are you crying?

MAGDALEN (*after a short pause; turning*). Sir, if you took the body of my Lord, would you kindly tell me where it is laid?

GARDENER (*after a pause*). Mary.

(*The scene has a compelling reality.* MAGDALEN *stares at the* GAR-DENER. *A low murmur ripples over the Court. Maybe it is only the suggestion of the acting. But the* GARDENER, *with his dark beard and face pale with excitement, has indeed taken on some resemblance to Jesus. Just the mirage of a second, but* MAGDALEN *cannot take her eyes from him. The Court batedly waits for her reaction. There is a pause, then* MAGDALEN *moves to the* GARDENER *and into the focus of the spotlight.*)

PROSECUTOR (*tensely*). Go on, Magdalen—fall on your knees—call him Master.

MAGDALEN (*with a start*). I won't fall on my knees—because he is not the Master!

PROSECUTOR (*easing to* L. *of* MAGDALEN). Take a better look—co-operate, Magdalen. Try to see with the same determination with which you wanted to see him before the tomb.

MAGDALEN (*turning to the* PROSECUTOR; *in cold rage*). Go away!

PROSECUTOR. Look at the light on his forehead. The shadows under his eyes. His pale skin, his dark beard—the face of your Jesus—the face of thousands in Jerusalem, in Galilee, in the world. All are sons of man—nothing but man. You might as well kneel down before him and call him Master.

MAGDALEN (*furiously*). Go away—don't you hear me—go away! You can't take away what I saw. If you take Jesus away from me, you take away my life—what I was born for—to see him. To tell that I saw him. You can't make me disbelieve my own eyes—to doubt the only truth I know. Don't tempt me. I know who you are. Go away, Devil!

PROSECUTOR (*smiling*). Imagination again, Magdalen. (*He crosses below* MAGDALEN *to* L. *of the* GARDENER *and faces* MAGDALEN.) I am no more Devil than he is Christ. You're afraid, aren't you? Not sure of yourself. You don't care to face the truth. Come, be courageous! Shake off this mad obsession. Open your eyes. Admit your mistake. (*He eases up* C.) Admit it was this gardener whom you met that morning.

MAGDALEN (*with a tortured cry*). He was not. . . . (*With full strength she hits the* GARDENER *full in the face.*)

(*The lights start to come up. The* COUNSELLOR *and the* GUARD *rise.*)

(*Hysterically.*) Would I dare to hit the image of the Master? Is that proof enough? Would I strike my Lord? (*She screams and hurls herself at the* GARDENER.) But I strike him—strike him—strike him. I won't stop until you will believe me.

(*In a blind frenzy she keeps hitting the* GARDENER *who stands paralyzed and takes the beating without a blink of his eyes, until* MAGDALEN *starts to collapse. Then he takes her protectively in his strong arms. For a moment, only her low sob is audible as her head is buried on the* GARDENER'S *chest.*)

PROSECUTOR (*moving down* L.). I have no more questions.
COUNSELLOR (*moving to* L. *of* MAGDALEN). Thank you, Magdalen for this testimony.

(MAGDALEN *recovers and looks around dazedly, only now realizing what she has done.*)

MAGDALEN (*to the* JUDGE). I have to apologize to the Court. (*To the* GARDENER.) And you, please—will you forgive me? I had to hit you for the glory of God.
JUDGE. The witness is excused.

(*The* GARDENER *leads* MAGDALEN *to the* GUARD, *then sits* R. *The* GUARD *ushers* MAGDALEN *to the door* R. *and opens it.* MAGDALEN *exits. The* GUARD *closes the door behind her and resumes his seat. The* PROSECUTOR *sits down* L.)

COUNSELLOR (*to the audience*). Ladies and gentlemen of the Jury —since the State is attempting to dismiss the Resurrection as the vision of an hysterical woman, I now call a witness who is not a woman, and certainly not hysterical. Mr Simon Peter.
GUARD (*rising, opening the door* R. *and calling*). Mr Simon Peter.

(SIMON PETER *enters* R., *and crosses above the* COUNSELLOR *to the witness stand. A fisherman, in oilskins, he is tall, broad-shouldered, face sunburned, bursting with vigour, and despite his white beard, very youthful and energetic. He has clear and serene eyes. He brings with him the bracing air of the sea. His simple joviality is very convincing.*)

COUNSELLOR. Will you take the stand, please.

(*After being sworn,* PETER *sits. The* GUARD *closes the door and sits.*)

Mr Simon Peter, did you meet the risen Jesus?
PETER. I did indeed, sir. We had dinner together Sunday evening.
COUNSELLOR. Are you positive that it was Jesus?

PETER. I am positive.

COUNSELLOR. Not a vision—not an apparition?

PETER. No, sir. We sat at the table with my whole crew. We had fish—broiled fish, the way he liked it.

COUNSELLOR. So he sat with you through the whole dinner?

PETER. Yes, sir, he did.

COUNSELLOR. Was that the only time you saw him?

PETER. No, sir. We ate with him again. And after that meeting even Thomas didn't doubt any longer. He touched the wounds.

COUNSELLOR. Thomas touched Jesus?

PETER. Yes—and was convinced. He exclaimed, "My Lord and my God!"

COUNSELLOR. How many appearances did he make among you?

PETER. Oh, later in Galilee he lived with us for weeks.

COUSELLOR (*perching himself on the* L. *side of his table down* R.). Please tell the Jury about this meeting in Galilee.

PETER (*expansively*). Well, sir, this is how it happened. One morning we went out on the lake. It was a fine day—good fishing weather. The wind blew from the Bethsaida corner—east wind. It blew a tide to the Galilean shore, and you know, fish go with the tide. So we didn't go far, just kept close to the shore. That's the way to fish, with an east wind. (*Expertly.*) Stay in shallow waters, let the nets hit the bottom, and wait. The wind will do the job. It drives the water right under your stern, and brings fish in schools. But just as we lowered the net, the wind suddenly stopped. There was such a calm, the water didn't even ripple. It was getting hot, and if my brow hadn't been sweating from the sun, I'd have said it was a frozen lake. And not a single fish—not even the scrubbiest little whitefish—nothing even worth throwing back in the water. (*He gives a little sigh.*) That was hard luck for all of us. I was getting kind of sore. You know, sometimes I have a bad temper. I just wanted to let go with a good healthy swearing, but then I remembered that I was the rock of the Church. John smiled at me. He was a bright boy. He always knew when I was about to lose my temper. "Let's wait," said John, "fish will come." "Let's go back," said Thomas, who never believed that anything would come. (*He gives a slight shrug of his shoulders.*) I decided to wait, but nothing stirred—the sea was dead. "What are we waiting for?" asked Thomas. "Fish," answered John, who never gave up. I was about to call off the whole thing when John cried out, "I see a herring!" Now I really got mad. Was he kidding me? It was the tiniest spot of a lake herring I've ever seen in my life—wasn't enough for the breakfast of a kitten. I had a good answer ready for John, when I remembered again my position, and didn't say a word. I just watched the sea—and suddenly, I saw a black streak on the clear waters. It looked like the shadow of a cloud—but there was not a single cloud in the sky. "Say, what's that?" I asked. "Fish," answered John, and smiled. And

he was right—it was fish. I tell you, sir, they just came as if on
order—and hurrying that they shouldn't be late. I never saw
such a thing before. They weren't afraid of us—they were eager
to be taken—just hurled themselves in the net. They simply
swamped us. (*Carried away, he relives the experience.*) "Come on,
boys," I shouted. "John, Thomas, Nathaniel, and all you others,
get up! This is it!" We jumped out of the boat, up to our waists
in the water, and began to draw the net. It almost broke it was so
heavy. "Heave ho, heave ho," I urged them on. (*He laughs.*) The
boat almost sank under the load. Fish gasping—flapping around
—silver scales glinting in the sunshine. It was a catch such as a
fisherman dreams of—a catch to tell your grandchildren about.
(*In ecstasy.*) Perch, pickerel, sturgeon, catfish, sucker, whitefish,
salmon and trout—bluebacks, yellow-fins, rainbows, steel-heads
—those with the large scales and thick skins, you know. And that
was only the half of it. The real big fellows were coming up—pike
and muakallungs—each a hundred and twenty pounds. Yes, sir,
that's how it happened. Pike, a hundred and twenty pounds. (*He
laughs.*) And not one, not two—dozens of those heavyweights.
"Thomas, why are you gaping? Let's go to work! We have a lot to
do. Cleaning, smoking, packing—we will ship them all over the
country. And there will be new boots, new shirts. We will mend
the roof for rainy days—and warm stockings—and food in the
larder—and next Passover, we won't offer a pigeon in the Temple
—we will offer a lamb!" (*He pauses.*) Then I suddenly stopped.
What an old fool I was! How slow on the uptake! I just took all
this for granted—business as usual—a regular thing to catch
those big ones in scores. Peter, Peter, I said to myself, you should
know better. This big catch must have some meaning—it must
be a sign—of something very, very great. Stop thinking of business, stockings, and food. Don't you see? It is a miracle! A miracle!
And then John cried out, "Peter, look!" I turned my head toward
the shore, (*very simply*) and there stood Jesus.

COUNSELLOR (*rising*). Jesus!

PETER. Yes, sir. That's how it happened.

COUNSELLOR. Thank you, Peter. That's all. (*He moves to his
chair down* R. *and sits.*)

PROSECUTOR (*rising; sarcastically*). A pretty fish story!

PETER (*indignantly*). I beg your pardon! Are you suggesting that
fishermen don't tell the truth? You'd better take my word!
(*Angrily.*) If I say a fish weighs a hundred and twenty pounds, you
can stake your life that it weighs a hundred and twenty pounds.
(*He rises and draws himself up to his full height, looking a giant among
the others. His voice thunders.*) And if I say he was the Lord, you may
fall on your knees, because he *was* the Lord.

(*There are some moments of silence, then the* PROSECUTOR *moves to* R. *of
his table and tries quickly to dispel the effect of* PETER'S *words.*)

Prosecutor (*maliciously*). If he was the Lord, why did he show himself only to hysterical women and garrulous fishermen?

(Saul *enters unobtrusively* r.)

Why didn't he appear before his enemies?

Saul (*moving* r.c.; *with the fervour of a man afire with the truth*). He did appear! He appeared before me!

(Saul's *sudden arrival is so compelling that the Court stares almost paralyzed.*)

You spoke the truth, Peter! He was the Lord! He lives! He is risen! I saw him!

(*The* Counsellor *rises.*)

Peter (*stunned*). *You* saw him? *You* who wanted to destroy him —and all of us.

Saul (*with passionate zeal*). I met him on the road to Damascus!

Peter (*puzzled*). But aren't you Saul of Tarsus?

Saul (*fiercely*). Saul of Tarsus is no more. (*He moves to* Peter.) I am Paul—come to confirm your words, Peter.

Peter. You are a Pharisee. You called us clumsy Galilean fishermen.

Saul. I did. Now I am a fish in your net—caught by Jesus—the Christ.

Peter (*reverently*). He made us fishers of men. You are a good catch, Paul of Tarsus. Speak up. Take my place.

(*He steps down from the witness stand, moves to the door* l. *and exits.* Saul *moves on to the stand and sits. The Court recovers and stirs excitedly.*)

Judge (*rapping with his gavel*). Order in the court.

Prosecutor. Your Honour, I didn't call back Saul of Tarsus.

Saul. Paul of Tarsus, if you please.

Prosecutor. Whatever you call yourself, you have no right to address this Court.

Counsellor. I call him as my witness. (*To* Saul.) Remain on the stand.

Saul. I have new testimony to give.

Prosecutor. I object! You have already given your testimony. You are no longer a witness here.

Judge. Objection overruled. The Court rules that the motion of the State be denied.

Prosecutor. Exception! (*He moves to his chair down* l. *and sits.*)

Judge (*with a sharp look at the* Prosecutor). The witness may continue.

Counsellor (*moving* c.). Tell us how you met the Lord.

Saul. It was high noon, and as I approached the gates of the

city, the road was drenched in white sunshine—stabbing and
gleaming like my hatred. My journey was nearing its end, and in
the distance I could see the towers of Damascus. My arrival there
would mean the end of the Christian community, and I was
burning, burning to carry out my task. Suddenly, I felt myself
wavering. I was seized by a power that struck me to earth, and as
I looked up—in a light that blinded me—I saw Jesus.

COUNSELLOR. The same Jesus you persecuted?

SAUL. And he asked my why. His voice was gentle and low, and
yet it echoed from all directions of the wind. Why? Why? Why?
Why persecute him? Why persecute anyone at all? And with all
my proud craft I couldn't answer that one humble question. I lay
in the dust defeated by the meek. I knew that I had always loved
him. Through his love, I was appointed.

COUNSELLOR. What was your mission?

SAUL. To testify. (*He rises.*) Your Honour, ladies and gentlemen
of the Jury, men and women of the world, Gentiles and Jews,
rulers and slaves—Jesus lives!

COUNSELLOR (*softly*). Thank you, Paul. (*He moves to his chair
down R. and sits. To the* PROSECUTOR.) Your witness.

(*The* PROSECUTOR *rises and moves* C. SAUL *sits.*)

PROSECUTOR. You testified that you were stricken blind. How
could you see the Lord?

SAUL. He struck me blind that I should see only him. He sent
me back into darkness—the darkness of the womb—and through
him I was born again.

PROSECUTOR (*sarcastically*). All this took place at noon, you said.
Did the sun stand high?

SAUL. At noon the sun always stands high.

PROSECUTOR. Was your head covered?

SAUL. If you're suggesting it was the sun—I admit it. But who
gave the sun power to strike me? The Lord Jesus! He struck Saul
to death and Paul was born.

PROSECUTOR (*bitingly*). But you testified that Jesus was a false
prophet.

SAUL. I changed my mind.

PROSECUTOR. The great opportunist.

SAUL. Yes, I grasped the great opportunity to save the world—
by giving the old word a new meaning. I'll carry this word to the
ends of the earth—every village, every town, every country,
every continent. I must reach all men, impregnate every soul—
teach, preach, write. . . .

PROSECUTOR (*sarcastically*). A press agent for God!

SAUL. God needs publicity. He's so well known that people
don't remember his name, and I am here to remind you that his
offer still stands—a guarantee of eternal life.

PROSECUTOR (*derisively*). And sealed by you, I presume.

SAUL (*humbly*). I am only a clerk—the seal was placed in Peter's hands. (*He rises, and turns to the* JUDGE.) And now, may I be excused? I have to catch the next boat. I have a long journey ahead of me—and each day may be the last.

PROSECUTOR. I have no more questions. (*He moves to his chair down* L. *and sits.*)

JUDGE. The witness is excused.

(SAUL *moves to the door* L. *with strong purposeful strides.*)

COUNSELLOR. *Bon voyage*, Paul of Tarsus.

(SAUL *exits.*)

JUDGE (*after a pause*). Are there any more witnesses?

COUNSELLOR (*rising*). Thousands of them, Your Honour—thousands through the ages—but I feel there is no need to call them. The Defence rests.

JUDGE. The Defence may begin its summation.

COUNSELLOR (*moving* C.; *to the audience*). Ladies and gentlemen—we will offer no summation. The implications of the testimony are plain. If you decide that the gardener stole the body, there is no resurrection. Our faith is in vain. Our love is meaningless. You, I, and all of us, stand stripped to the bone, exposed to brutal physical law. (*He gives a slight bow.*) I ask for a verdict of—not guilty. (*He moves to his chair down* R. *and sits.*)

(*The* PROSECUTOR *rises and moves* C.)

PROSECUTOR (*to the audience*). May it please the Court—ladies and gentlemen of the Jury, the implications of the testimony are indeed very plain. A body disappeared. The Defence would have you believe that it disappeared by means of a miracle. A pitiful attempt to obscure the fact that all this was a well-calculated plot. Many witnesses tried to refute my accusation, but the one witness who could do so was not produced. I mean, the living Jesus. (*He gives a slight bow.*) I ask for a verdict of—guilty, as charged. (*He moves to his chair down* L. *and sits.*)

JUDGE (*after a pause*). Ladies and gentlemen of the Jury—you have heard the evidence. You must bear in mind that the accused is presumed wholly innocent until proved guilty beyond reasonable doubt. The State has produced not a single eye-witness who saw the gardener steal the body, and its contention is based principally on the fact that the tomb was empty—a point on which both counsels agree. (*He pauses.*) On the other hand, no testimony has been offered of having seen Jesus in the very act of rising. No Defence witness saw him walking out of his grave. But they saw a man walking in the garden—on the seashore—on the road—and firmly testified that he was the same Jesus of Nazareth who died on the cross. (*Emphatically.*) However, the mere fact that these reported events appear to be in the realm of

the supernatural, doesn't give justification to the Jury for doubt-
ing the witnesses' integrity. In the opinion of the Court, this evidence is not a question of belief or disbelief—it is a question of
what testimony is worth in itself. This testimony before us is no
less valid and no more doubtful than any testimony in any trial
in any other case—and it should be regarded as such. (*He leans
forward over his desk.*) Therefore, this Court instructs you, ladies
and gentlemen of the Jury, that in weighing the facts, you should
not be influenced by any preference or prejudice. You must not
believe *any* part of this testimony for the sole reason that it sounds
feasible. But at the same time, you must not disbelieve any part of
it *only* because it sounds miraculous. Every moment of our life is a
miracle, though performed within the frame of so-called physical
laws. But I advise you not to depend on it too strongly—because
we still don't know what physical law is. It might be weaker than
illusion. (*Matter of factly.*) Thus, your duty, ladies and gentlemen,
is reduced to finding one answer—why was the tomb empty on the
third day? And in this search, no-one can help you—for man is
created to labour on the truth, and carry the burden of making
his own decision. Only deep reflection can guide you to a just
verdict.

(*The light of dawn and the rising sun begins to appear through the
windows.*)

(*He glances out of the windows and smiles faintly.*) It is a good day for
reflection. Dawn, which will end this, our Vigil, is breaking over
the town. People are awakening, stretching after the night—
going out—walking in the growing light. The air is fresh and
clean.
(*The distant sound of church bells is heard.*)

The streets are newly swept. Church doors are open, sunrise
service begins on the hills. The grass is green—seeds are stirring.
It is spring——
(*The light of the rising sun grows stronger.*)

—it is Easter Morning. (*He pauses.*) Ladies and gentlemen of the
Jury, have you considered your verdict?
CLERK (*rising*). We have, Your Honour.
JUDGE. Deliver it to the Court.

*Through the window there drifts in softly, the sound of an organ and a
choir singing, "Jesus Christ is risen today, Alleluia." Then the sound
of the bells increases, the voices rise jubilantly and the sunlight streams in
as—*

the CURTAIN *slowly falls.*

FURNITURE AND PROPERTY LIST

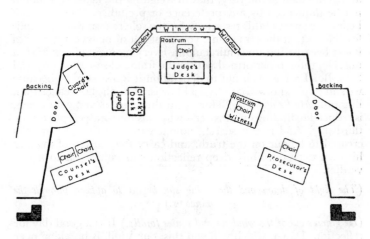

Rostrum (up C.).
Desk (JUDGE). *On it:* **inkstand,** pens, law books, papers, gavel.
High-backed chair.
Rostrum (L.C.).
Chair (WITNESS).
Desk (CLERK). *On it:* law books, papers, pens, inkstand.
2 Tables. *On them:* law books, papers.
5 Chairs.
Pail, mop, broom, dust-pan (up L.).
Duster.
Bunch of keys.

LIGHTING PLOT

ACT I

To open. Lights checked to ½.
Sunset effect behind windows.

Cue 1. At rise of CURTAIN.
Commence slow dim to ½.

Cue 2. As watchman exits.
Quick dim to black-out.

Cue 3. CLERK: This Court is now in session.
Raise lights of courtroom gradually to full. Blue outside windows.

Cue 4. SAUL exits.
Quick dim to black-out.

ACT II

To open. All lights out.

Cue 1. At rise of CURTAIN.
Raise lights of courtroom gradually to full. Blue outside windows.

Cue 2. MAGDALEN: Life—everlasting.
Quick dim to black-out.

ACT III

To open. All lights out.

Cue 1. At rise of CURTAIN.
Raise lights of courtroom gradually to full. Blue outside windows.

Cue 2.   PROSECUTOR: His shadow fell upon the grass.
           All lights checked to ¼ except a Spotlight off R.,
           focussed on the GARDENER.

Cue 3.   MAGDALEN strikes the GARDENER.
           Raise lights gradually to full.

Cue 4.   JUDGE: . . . guide you to a just verdict.
           Commence slow sunrise through windows.